G000136617

Snakes and Ladder

SNAKES AND LADDERS

HELENA WILKINSON

RoperPenberthy Publishing Ltd
Horsham, England

Published by RoperPenberthy Publishing Ltd
PO Box 545, Horsham, England RH12 4QW
www.roperpenberthy.co.uk

ISBN 978-1-903905-28-9

Cover design by Angie Moyler

Typeset by Avocet Typeset, Chilton, Aylesbury, Bucks
Printed in the United Kingdom by
J. H. Haynes and Co. Ltd., Sparkford, Somerset

CONTENTS

The Lord is close to those who are of a broken heart
(Psalm 34:18a, The Amplified Bible)

But those who trust in the LORD for help
will find their strength renewed.
They will rise on wings like eagles;
they will run and not get weary,
they will walk and not grow weak.
(Isaiah 40:31, GNB)

In memory of Guy and Jan Daynes,
faithful servants of God.

On 1 December 2006, at my place of work, Nicholaston House, I was participating in the annual event, *Countdown to Christmas*. One of the other participants, whom I didn't know, came up to me afterwards. 'Does the name Jan Daynes mean anything to you?' he asked. 'Yes,' I replied as I reflected on my involvement with Guy and Jan some twenty years previously and how that day I had been looking over the manuscript of this very book, in which Guy and Jan play a significant part. Nigel explained that he was a good friend of Guy and Jan Daynes and that he and I had been in correspondence in the mid 1980s when Guy and Jan had told him about me and consequently he'd reviewed my books, *Puppet on a*

String and *Snakes and Ladders* in a GP journal. Twenty years on, here we were now only living a few miles apart and reading at the same Christmas event!

'Did you know that Jan died a few months ago?' Nigel asked. I didn't.

Guy had died a couple of years previously – both had lived long lives and dedicated many, many years to helping those in need in rural Southern Africa. Their faith, service and actions changed the lives of numerous people including my own.

Snakes and Ladders

Play the game
beware mistakes,
it's up the ladders
not down the snakes.
Throw the dice
but don't just sit,
fight the pull
of the snake in his pit,
lest you should slide
all the way down
and lose your chance
of gaining a crown.
For the snake is
Satan in disguise,
the ladder, the steps
to our heavenly prize.

Age 22

INTRODUCTION

For the greater part of my teens I found myself caught in the depths of anorexia nervosa, an illness that tore my body and mind apart and left me emaciated, fearful and in deep depression. It was a visible expression of unresolved emotional conflict, inner pain and a resulting inability to cope with everyday life.

In coming to know God and eventually putting my trust in Him I was able to find release from the torment of the eating disorder mindset, and discover new purpose and meaning in life. With the illness barely over I recorded all that I had been through in my first book, *Puppet on a String*, in an attempt to offer hope and comfort to other sufferers and insight for family and friends.

At the time, people probably thought I was being presumptuous in saying that I felt sure *Puppet* would be accepted for publication. My reason for saying this was that I knew God was the one who had prompted me to write it in the first place, despite still being a teenager and having just failed my English Language exams for the second time! (*Puppet on a String* became a bestseller and remains in print more than twenty years later!)

A few years after *Puppet on a String* hit the market and proved to be so popular I was asked to write a sequel, as many people having read the book wanted to know if I had sustained recovery. I *had* sustained recovery and as I encountered various other experiences I began to see that suffering can become a privilege which bears fruit.

It was the knowledge of this privilege and my desire to light sparks of encouragement and comfort in those still caught in the trap of physical and emotional pain that allowed me once more to share of myself in a manuscript. This manuscript, which I called *Snakes and Ladders*, was written nearly twenty years ago, but I have chosen to allow it to go into print again as I feel that some of its content may be of benefit to those who are in the place I was at during the time of writing. I made the decision to edit the manuscript very little, despite having moved on vastly in my reflections on my life and in biblical understanding, because I feel to alter what I wrote at a young age might take away the heart behind the words.

The theme of *Snakes and Ladders* is that of Romans 8:28, *We know that in all things God works for good with those who love him, those whom he has called according to his purpose* (GNB). *Snakes and Ladders* is about the ups and downs of life. What I hope to reveal is that whether we are climbing up the ladder or sliding down the snake, God is just as real. He has a plan and purpose for each of our lives, and whatever the circumstances His love for us does *not* change. *The LORD'S unfailing love and mercy still continue, fresh as the morning, as sure as the sunrise* (Lamentations 3:22-23, GNB).

It took a long time for me to realise the unconditional love of God; it took even longer to see that the strength of my faith need not be dependent on the state of my emotions. One of my favourite verses in the Bible says, *My grace is sufficient for you, for my power is made perfect in weakness* (2 Corinthians 12:9, RSV). It was in times of great weakness that I acknowledged the importance of dying to self and was most able to see God at work. With hindsight I can see that it was not when life was going well that most lessons were learned or my character was formed – it was during the times of choking in the mud of suffering at the bottom of a black pit. Only now am I able to be thankful for the harder moments, and I believe that had I not taken that step of commitment to God at the time, I would still be bitterly resenting every bad incident in my life. I also feel sure that I would not have come through the anorexia. Maybe the words of an old school friend would be true, 'I doubt you would even be alive'.

One of Paul E Bilheimer's books has the wonderful title, *Don't Waste Your Sorrows*. My motto is 'Don't wallow in your suffering, but don't waste your sorrows'.

I hope that *Snakes and Ladders* will make you both laugh and cry, and that it will move you and challenge you and stimulate much thought. If through my words I touch the heart and life of even one person, then I consider my efforts, and my decision to reprint the manuscript, to have been worthwhile.

Helena Wilkinson, Swansea 2006

1

Where the hyena laughs

Where the hyena laughs
the sun is warm
and skies are often blue.
Snakes slither across
the hardened earth
and lions prowl around
looking for food;
buck run through
dry brown grass
and hippos sink into
muddy pools and wallow.
At night the moon hovers
over grey-blue mountains
and casts its eerie light;
crickets begin their
high-pitched buzz,
large cats call with
piercing cries and
tribesmen sit in huts.
In towns, rich and poor
both walk the streets
but sadly the hungry
wither in the heat,
their swollen bellies
dying to be filled.
Children are left to play
in red dust roads

and can be seen to
smile or cry in agony.
Where the hyena laughs
I was born,
and one day shall
return.

'Ruth,' I whispered, 'Are you awake?'

'Mm.'

'Ruth, there's a hyena lying against my leg.'

'Don't be so stupid, go back to sleep.'

'I'm telling you, there's a hyena lying against my leg.'

'Sure there is!'

My words were slower and more pronounced as I repeated for the third time what I had said. There was a moment's silence, then she turned to face me.

'You're kidding!'

'No, I'm serious,' I said.

'Oh!'

To my horror I realised that my fearless sister might actually have been as scared as I was, and had nothing to say. We had been foolish enough to pitch our tent right beside the animals' night-path to liquid refreshment!

For what seemed an age I had lain awake listening to the distant cries of large cats and hearing the sniffing and scratching of hyenas on the scrounge for scraps of food. If only our companions had been more careful in throwing their leftovers onto the fire! I didn't dare think what might happen if one of the hyenas smelt food inside our tent. Suddenly the sniffing had stopped and I had felt a warm lump pressing against my leg. Fear flooded my body. Why did the hyena have to choose me? Minutes seemed like hours and I wondered how long I could lie motionless on the hard, rocky ground. At last I felt the pressure on my leg released and breathed a sigh of relief!

Until that moment the reality of my vulnerability had not sunk in: I was still mesmerised by the sounds and atmosphere of 'darkest' Africa.

Camping in the bush in Kenya was proving to be a love-hate experience although something for which Ruth and I had longed for many years. We had chosen to explore the country of our birth, Kenya, on my way to do voluntary work in a Zulu hospital in a rural part of South Africa.

I had spent a good part of the flight from London to Nairobi contemplating what the following year would bring as I watched a liquid pink sun being consumed by the golden sands of the Sahara Desert. Stepping out of the aeroplane onto the arid African soil a whole new world lay before me.

Being on safari was the start of this new world – not only wild animals but wild people too! Ruth and I were the only girls (I was twenty-two and Ruth twenty-five). Our companions consisted of three heavy-drinking, middle-aged and rather coarse Scotsmen, two Northerners in their twenties (one looked very strange) and a Canadian guy who was quite obviously on drugs; then there were the African guide and cook.

Sex discrimination was out, and I began to see why all our companions were male when we were sent out in the heat to gather huge fallen branches for firewood, carefully checking each piece for snakes before dragging it away with our rough and blistered hands.

The wood was stacked in a large pile and as darkness swallowed the land, so roaring orange flames engulfed the logs. We drew close and sat in a circle around the fire to eat the evening meal which our cook had prepared. Tough, charred meat and boiled potatoes taste the same the world over, except when you are in the bush and ravenous: then anything tastes good!

Relaxing round the campfire in the security of its light often made a peaceful end to an active day. One night, though, we had an encounter which was far from peaceful. Returning to camp after several hours of game-drive we discovered that two elephants had lodged themselves amongst our belongings. They had chosen our camp as their route and, being stubborn creatures, nothing was going to convince them that they were not welcome. They stood in all splendour between the long-drop toilets and the tent Ruth and I shared. Our guide climbed into the van, headlights full on and horn in action. It was fine for him inside the van but not so fine for us standing in the dark staring at two huge bodies silhouetted between the dazzling light and ourselves, knowing that there was nowhere to run except into the bush where lion and hyena were lurking!

The days proved interesting, as we ploughed our way through the sticky mud, seeing an amazing variety of animals, but the nights became increasingly unwelcome. We were plagued by thunder, lightning, torrential rain and raging winds. We found ourselves desperately clinging to the tent-pole to stop the tent taking off. My nerves weren't helped either when just before going to bed one night I stumbled across a buffalo skull just behind our tent. The gruesome thought crossed my mind that we could end up in the same sorry state. However, the antics of monkeys and baboons kept us too well amused to allow me to dwell on such thoughts. They are bold animals and always up to something. One evening our funny little cook, with a yellow tea-cosy on his head, was trying to prepare the meal, but as fast as he peeled potatoes they were stolen by mischievous monkeys above! He shouted and stamped his feet, his little old face screwing up like a creased cloth and his too-short bell-bottom trousers swaying in his rage. The monkeys made themselves scarce, watching from a distance in eager anticipation, only to pounce again when his back was turned.

Encounters with wild animals were one thing but seeing at close quarters the Masai tribe who still live a primitive, nomadic lifestyle proved equally fascinating and occasionally alarming.

Along the escarpment of the Rift Valley where monkeys play and leopards have been seen, down rough red roads, there is the Kedong Masai Manyatta. A semi-circle of low, dung-plastered huts, surrounded by a thorn bush barrier, nestles amongst lush vegetation. Children amuse themselves on the dusty, manure-smelling earth and women sit making bracelets and necklaces from brightly-coloured beads, and creating water carriers from huge dried gourds. It was difficult for us to believe that people still had such primitive lifestyles, making mud-huts and drinking a mixture of milk and blood which they carefully siphoned out of the cattle they kept, without having to take the animal's life.

There were lion dances and Masai battle practices being carried out by dozens of tall, lean men whose hair and skin were stained red by a mixture of pulverised animal fat and the red earth, and whose bodies had pieces of red cloth thrown around them.

After the dancing was over the women displayed all their craftwork, eager that we should buy from them – bracelet after bracelet was placed on our arms at tremendous speed until each arm was a plaster-cast of multi-coloured beads. As we tried to take bracelets off more were added. We both left on our arms the few bracelets we chose to buy and handed back what remained, resisting the instance that we had to have this one and this one as well.

In need of space from the pressing bodies, I wandered off on my own. Peace at last! In minutes a tall, lean warrior approached me and with great pride showed me his spear. I made signs of approval. The warrior pointed to my watch and his face lit up. He wanted to exchange his spear for my watch! I liked the spear, it would have made an excellent souvenir but on the other hand I needed my watch – how could I do without it in my new job in South Africa! Within that split second of hesitation at least a dozen other warriors had congregated around me, all thrusting their spears in my direction. I looked around, stunned, as I realised that I was like an insect caught in a web – a web of closely-knit warriors and spears. All eyes were focused on my wrist! Thoughts floated through my mind: how was I going to tackle telling these people that I would really rather hang onto the watch myself, especially if in doing so I ran the risk of a dozen spears through my chest! I didn't relish the thought of death just yet!

How things had changed; less than six years ago I had been lying in a hospital bed too weak even to walk, fighting against anorexia nervosa and willing death to come and steal away the pain. Now I was fighting fit and raring to go, and death was the last of my wishes. I thought too of how afraid I would have been in such a situation and the difference God has made to my self-confidence in the four years of being a Christian.

The thudding of spears on the ground quickly brought me back to the here and now – I was still imprisoned in my cage of warriors. What was I going to say? I pointed to my watch, shook my head from side to side and smiled. No hard feelings, bodies moved away like the parting of the waters and I stepped out. What a relief!

I had for a split second felt trapped with the warriors, although in my heart of hearts I felt they meant no harm. However, my experience of my safari companions left no doubt that I was at risk. Not only did I have the safari guide making continuous passes but I was targeted by those in the group. One night I found myself the only one not taking drugs. When even my sister accepted to smoke marihuana, I became the odd one out. We were all sitting round the camp fire, recounting the escapades of the day. The next thing I knew was that I was being dragged back to my tent, unable to feel my legs. The men had drugged my drink and I had lost consciousness. I had no idea for how long or what had happened during that time. Once in the tent I felt so ill. One of the men returned with the guide. Realising I was still not right they debated, and then declined, taking me to hospital some 100 miles across rough bush. The night was rough as I could hardly move. The next day I lay in my tent in the scorching heat, not knowing fully what had happened the previous night; I cried out to God to have mercy and I felt so utterly alone. What would I have done without the Lord, I couldn't imagine.

Back in Nairobi the streets seemed crowded and cluttered after our days on safari and the vast expanse of bush. On the outskirts of Nairobi were the shanty towns: dozens of dilapidated shacks with tin roofs as homes, so closely packed together there was hardly walking space between them. Ragged clothes hung on lines strung between crumbling walls and children sat at the edge of the road amongst the litter and the dust staring hopelessly into thin air, their eyes too large for their heads, torn cloth hanging on their frail bodies: emaciated arms outstretched. I longed to bend down, gather them in my arms and hold them tight.

One glance at such sights and I knew that I would never be the same again. Never again could I be envious of those who have more than I have or who have an easier life. Never again could I not be grateful for the food I have to nourish me and keep my body healthy. As I felt the pain of poverty I realised what Jesus meant when He said that it is harder for a rich man to enter the kingdom of God than for a camel to pass through the eye of a needle. Even I, with the little I had, was rich compared with these people who had nothing to come between them and God.

Such sights faded into the distance, but not out of my memory, as Ruth and I chugged along on the night train from Nairobi to Mombassa. We had decided to visit the coastal area where we had spent our first holidays as youngsters, with our parents.

After a restless night, with the stopping and starting of the train, we woke to the sound of a xylophone being played to announce that breakfast was ready. As we pulled into Mombassa station there was no mistaking that we were at the coast – the land was littered with palm trees and the high humidity hit us as soon as we stepped out of the train. Taxi-men swarmed around us shouting, 'Taxi, taxi,' and I longed to escape the over-powering crowds and heat to sit in a pool of cool water by myself. We had learnt through experience that you haggle over taxi prices and once we had made a good deal we set off to catch the Likoni ferry. The ferry was just drawing out as we arrived and so we thrust our money into the taxi-man's hand, ran at speed and jumped on board. To our disbelief a car followed close behind and sped onto the already moving ferry too! That's Africa!

At Likoni we found a local bus that was going to Diani Beach, our destination. People piled onto the bus with bags, bursting at the seams: an abundance of bananas, coconuts and other fruits. Had there been any chickens they would have been squeezed on too. The bus was packed with sweaty bodies; the odour overwhelming. Everyone on the bus was Asian or African and people stared at us mystified as to why two white girls were travelling alone on such primitive transport. In their eyes our affluence could have afforded us the luxury of a taxi; in our eyes we wanted to save our pennies for better things. We had chosen to sit at the back of the bus and wondered why everyone else appeared to be avoiding it. The reason was that the roads were full of pot-holes the size of ditches, the bus had little suspension and every time we hit a bump our spines almost pierced our brains! After an hour of experiencing life as an overheated milkshake we finally arrived at Diani Beach. There in front of us sat our little white guest house nestling in vivid pink bougainvillea and looking out across the turquoise Indian Ocean.

When the tide was out it exposed an expanse of rugged rocks and limp seaweed. We stumbled over the rocks to the brilliant white sand where we met a young African who offered to take us out in his boat, little more than a hollowed-out tree trunk. The water was clear and sparkled like crystal in the sunlight. Leaving the boat at the edge of the reef we carried our goggles and snorkels to the other side to explore the deep, wide ocean and its underwater world. It was beautiful with coral formations of intricate design, multi-coloured fish and fans of weed gently swaying. This was tranquillity and luxury in its fullest form and the only price I had to pay was a lobster-like body and peeling skin.

Walking back to the guest house we were stopped by one of the African workers who was keen to take us to his native village. We piled into a matatu (a very cheap means of transport used by the Africans which is crammed full of bodies) and alighted beside a row of wooden shacks selling meat, vegetables, tropical fruits and sodas.

As we wandered deeper into Ukunda and neighbouring villages we saw women with babies strapped to their backs pounding their washing in murky water. Children playing in the dry earth leapt with excitement when they saw us. They followed behind us crocodile-fashion repeatedly shouting, 'Wazungu, wazungu,' (White people, white people).

Passing the mud houses with their straw roofs we noticed how the women were fastidious and house-proud in their own way. As the sun sank lower and the day drew to a close they took to tidying their homes; one took a broom, consisting of a bundle of sticks, and swept away the rubbish which had collected in the little yard. Dozens of complaining hens were caught up in the clouds of dust and fled squawking. A woman with a sick baby on her back carried out a wooden table, placed a sheet over it and set up her charcoal-heated iron. She dragged down from the straw roof the clothes she had laid out to dry and started her work.

People smiled and greeted us with warm welcomes; their joy at having us in their village was unmistakably genuine.

Life was basic, but it was difficult to decide whether such an existence was simplicity or poverty.

It seemed unbelievable that this country of contrasts was where I was born, and after our coast break at Diani Beach was over, Ruth and I went on a two-hour nostalgia trip when we returned to where we used to live, the research station at Muguga, a short distance from Nairobi. The house seemed completely different from family photographs. It still looked out across the Ngong Hills, but that was about all that remained the same. It was in poor condition and the garden that my parents had spent hours creating, with its outdoor stage, lily beds and artistic landscape, was little more than a jungle of grass and weeds. Twenty-two years had passed to steal away the beauty and although I was disappointed with what I saw, I simultaneously felt a warm glow inside. It was not simply nostalgia but a rediscovery of the first few months of my life; as though visiting the place of my birth enabled me to find some missing pieces of the jigsaw of my life.

There was so much of my past of which I had little or no recollection and yet I knew that it had a significant bearing on the formation of my character, and my reactions during teenage years. Somehow, standing on African soil emphasised the reality of what I had been told of my early years and helped me to understand my deep fears of rejection.

From the start, life had been a struggle. Starved in the womb by the umbilical cord being very thin and twisted around my neck, I was born a week early at a low weight, and after which I was shunted many times between hospital and home and denied the chance of much maternal love and care. In the months which followed, the discovery of a serious eye defect resulted in being hospitalised again, and undergoing a general anaesthetic. All this coincided with our move to England.

It seemed that unfortunate circumstances and events came to steal and disrupt the love process. The death of one of my closest school friends when I was seven, on-going experiences of sexual and emotional abuse and the physical and emotional bullying I received later at boarding school, reinforced my growing need for love and yet my feelings of being unlovable.

Looking back I realise that right from childhood days the 'snakes and ladders' pattern was in existence. At times it may have seemed as though life was one long series of sliding down the snakes, but with hindsight I can see God's loving plan for my life. Returning to Kenya was one of the most significant parts of that plan, as was my going on to do voluntary work in South Africa.

My time of revisiting Kenya had come to an end and as I sat on the plane from Nairobi to Johannesburg, contemplating what the next year would bring in another foreign land, I closed my eyes and recalled some of the experiences I had been through in the years between writing *Puppet on a String* and my decision to venture into work in Zululand. As I did so I realised how God had so often used painful times to challenge my outlook on life and draw me closer to Him.

2

The arrow

I watch an arrow being fired,
Its long slender body
Cuts through thin air
With ease and grace.
Its painfully pointed end
Faces my direction
But travels so fast so swiftly
I have no time to move;
Too short a time to count.
Even a second's too great,
I can only sit and stare
As it pierces my skin
And forces its way in.
Yet I feel nothing at all.
My body's numb, senseless,
Frozen to the bone.
I watch the arrow bury itself
Deeper and deeper
But still I feel no pain;
Then a sudden agony takes hold,
Gripping, even crippling
And I know it's reached my heart,
But who can tell?
For it leaves no signs,
No blood, no mess,
Nothing visible for friend
To see or comprehend;

Simply sits embedded
In heart and soul
And allows for silent suffering.

One of the more painful experiences I recalled was the death of my cousin. Kathie had become very special to me because in times of loneliness and despair at boarding school she was the only person in whom I had been able to confide. Although parted by the thousands of miles between England and Bermuda, where she lived, the ties of family drew us close. Being older, she could tell me stories of the grandparents I never really knew and so help to give me a sense of belonging. She was like an older sister and a mother-figure to me and people even commented that we looked alike!

Her death, only a few months after I had finished writing *Puppet on a String*, remains one of the most traumatic and yet significant events of my life.

The evening service at my local church, Greyfriars, had just ended. I was talking and laughing amongst my friends, when I saw my parents walking towards me. It was unusual for them to be at Greyfriars Church. I smiled and waved. The crowds of people were streaming towards the door, but my parents were pushing against the tide and ushering me back into a pew. I looked into their eyes, and saw a pained expression. The church was almost empty now and I sensed that their souls were empty too. Organ music played quietly in the background and my father turned to me with equal softness.

'Uncle Jack phoned.'

A thousand thoughts ran through my mind.

'It's some very sad news about Kathie.'

'She hasn't got cancer has she?' I asked.

But before I had even realised what I had said his answer hit me hard and shattered my entire being into a million pieces.

'I'm afraid Kathie's dead, love.'

The word 'dead' resounded in the empty building and I felt an arrow pierce my body and bury itself deep inside my heart.

There was a cold silence.

Then suddenly the arrow was pulled from my heart with tremendous force causing unbearable pain. All that remained was a dark void.

'No!' I yelled.

A flood of tears surged forward and my body was caught on the waves of disbelief which thrashed around, striking and throwing me from rock to rock until I was completely numb to reality.

I struggled to fight the many emotions which were crowding in upon me like a mass of tangled weeds, suffocating and choking, and ask my parents how it all happened. No one knew for certain what had caused Kathie's death, just that her body had been found in the bath with much of the flesh burned off from scalding water – all evidence washed away.

We stood up and walked out of the church; everything was a blur. It felt as if I was trapped in a nightmare and my body refused to gain consciousness. This was unbelievable; it had to be a dream. The Vicar shook my hand warmly as we made our way into the West End for coffee. If it wasn't a dream, there must have been some terrible mistake; Kathie had only written to me a few weeks ago inviting me to stay for Christmas. She couldn't be dead; I had just accepted her invitation. She had helped me through many a personal crisis and I always told myself, 'Whatever happens, at least I know

Kathie's always there.' Now she was gone for ever. How did they know it was her body that had been found? Who had identified her?

My tear-stained eyes skimmed the crowd; where was Joan, the Vicar's wife? I had to speak with her; she'd understand the intensity of the pain which flowed like a gushing river. She had walked along dark paths with me before and many a time had carried on where Kathie had left off, helping me to cope with negative emotions and encouraging me to place everything in God's hands.

Joan pulled up a chair and sat down beside me whilst my parents went to fetch some coffee. It wasn't necessary for her to say much; all I needed was empathy and I knew for certain that I had this. My parents joined us and in our little circle we shared moments of weeping, moments of silence and moments of inadequate words. For most of the time my head hung low, eyes fixed on the black trousers that I was wearing, following the fine corduroy lines up and down. I was dressed in black and red and a bright red poppy stood out against my pale cream jacket. It was Remembrance Sunday – a time when the loss of loved ones was uppermost in people's minds. I had just sung hymns about those who had passed through the veil between this life and the next, and prayed for others who were suffering bereavement. Not once did I think that tonight I would be suffering the same thing.

It had been an active day and as usual I had been rushing around. My final rush was to get to the church on time; I had arranged to meet with Joan before the service to pray about a new job I was to start the next day. Our praying together had been very special; more special that I could imagine, since what I did not realise was that Joan already knew about Kathie's death. My mother had telephoned her a few hours previously to ask for her prayers. The prayers she prayed when we met together and the Bible verse she had written out for me were to uphold me not just as I faced a new and challenging job, but also a great loss.

Sitting stony-faced, I glanced again at the verse. *Fear not; (there is nothing to fear) for I am with you; do not look around you in terror and be dismayed, for I am your God. I will strengthen and harden you (to difficulties); yes, I will help you; yes, I will hold you up and retain you with My victorious right hand of rightness and justice* (Isaiah 41:10, The Amplified Bible). The words gave me strength and courage, as did Joan's final prayer before stepping out into the bitter cold November night.

The eight-mile journey to my parents' home seemed to have taken an eternity, but it was far better to have their company than to be alone in my bed-sit, even though it meant an added seven miles. My tense body started to feel awkward in the soft chair. There were things that needed to be done – close friends of Kathie's to phone, who I felt sure would not yet know. If I didn't do it straightaway I'd lose the courage. Hesitantly I picked up the receiver and dialled … Unable to believe the words I had just spoken I knew I had to close my eyes to the truth. Sleep eluded me; but by weeping until too exhausted to carry on, the curtain of sleep was finally drawn.

My first day at work came and went. I was one of fourteen young people working on a project to set up and run crèches attached to adult education centres in Reading, particularly English language classes for Asian and West Indian families. It didn't take long to see the frustration and hard work involved; three people resigned on the first day and several others spoke of doing so. I spent the entire eight hours wandering around like a zombie.

Back at home I poured over photos of times I had shared with Kathie. I desperately tried to relive the events and atmosphere which the pictures had captured. Once again I felt the hot Bermuda sun beat down on my back and the fine pink sand move between my toes. I watched the turquoise sea lash against the limestone rock, heard the melodious song of the yellow bird way up in the banana tree and the swish of the gracious palms swaying in the wind. I walked along narrow streets past pastel-coloured houses capped with white limestone roofs and touched luscious hedgerows over-flowing with pink hibiscus flowers, and I breathed in the tangy scent of the citrus trees heavily laden with fruit. But most of all I talked; I spoke the same words I had spoken ten months ago when working through inner pain and turmoil, and I listened to the same advice.

I heard Kathie's last words before stepping on to the plane and trading subtropical sea and sand for a snow-capped city, 'I'll see you in England soon'.

'Soon' had passed in only a few weeks and we had an addition to our family; after spending nine years in Bermuda Kathie had chosen to move back to England. With no parents, our house became her home until she moved to Chester and found a job teaching art.

Before the school term began she invited me to stay. Going to Chester brought about tremendous feelings of nostalgia – it was around this area that much of my father's side of the family had their roots. All the stories that Kathie used to tell me in letters about Grandma and Grandpa and their little dog, Rusty, started to come alive as we roamed the streets and visited family houses. Our last visit took us on the bus from Chester to Waverton, the small village where our grandparents used to live. Before leaving Waverton Kathie asked if I would like to see the church and graveyard where they were buried. We sat beside the grave pressing back in the lead letters which had fallen out. A golden sun shone on the mass of delicate wild flowers and Kathie recalled one of the stories she had told me a few years ago about going to stay with Grandma and Grandpa.

'It was like going back in time a century, with all the photos of our ancestors on the wall in the hallway, the summer house in the garden and the orchard in which

Grandpa gave us our own apple tree. I can still picture him carving the Sunday joint, sitting in his armchair at the table, and going to the shops with me and Rusty, the dog, who could do just about anything. It is a pity that you didn't know Grandpa; he was a wonderful man.'

We stood up and walked around the corner to her mother's grave. I felt Kathie's body tense up as she spoke of how cold that grey stone cross seemed to her. Her restlessness portrayed a sense of urgency, as though she did not want to stay there long. We turned round and left. This was the last time I was to see Kathie and she had taken me to visit her own grave. Three months later I walked that same patch of grass and watched the wooden coffin being lowered into the ground. This time there was no August sun to warm me, only an icy December wind which ate deep into my body.

The funeral service had helped me to accept that Kathie was really dead; the act of seeing the coffin covered in wreaths and hearing the vicar speak of her short life now passed; singing the hymns I had chosen and hearing the words of comfort read from Scripture.

> *The Lord is my shepherd, I shall not want;*
> *He makes me lie down in green pastures.*
> *He leads me beside still waters,*
> *He restores my soul.*
> *He leads me in paths of righteousness*
> *for his name's sake.*
>
> *Even though I walk through the valley*
> *of the shadow of death,*
> *I fear no evil;*
> *for thou art with me;*
> *thy rod and thy staff,*
> *they comfort me.*

(Psalm 23; 1-4, RSV)

Understanding that Kathie was dead was one thing, but death held a finality about it which was totally unacceptable. A finality that even time was powerless to change. There was nothing which could bring Kathie back; nothing which could alter the situation and as one week faded into another so disbelief and pain merged into anger and guilt. Anger that God could have allowed such a tragedy to happen; guilt over actions I had lived to regret and words I had longed to say which death had now ruthlessly stolen from me.

Added to all the usual emotions which bereavement brings was the complete inability to let go and accept what had happened, for the simple reason that more than six months after Kathie had died the inquest into her death had still not been concluded and all that had happened remained an utter mystery.

My personality is such that I need conclusion; I cannot handle uncertainty and not knowing why or how Kathie had died was tearing me to pieces. There was talk of suicide, murder, 'natural causes'. How could I live whilst the papers printed horrific facts, without concrete evidence, that instilled fear and revulsion in me and destroyed any chance of peace of mind? Physically I could feel something gnawing away inside my body and the emotions that pulsed through my veins were filled with deadly poison. The strain was beginning to take its toll and I began to feel that if something did not happen soon to ease the agony, I would crack. I began to pray that the inquest would be concluded very soon and whatever the verdict I would be satisfied and able to let go.

Nine months after Kathie had died, the results of the inquest came through the post. The verdict was accidental death. It was said that the coroner, who was very sympathetic, was forced into this decision really by a process of elimination but that despite extensive medical tests having been carried out no cause of death had been found. The coroner said that the reason it happened could only be conjecture and that sadly it would remain one of life's mysteries.

Although it still remained a mystery, God graciously answered my prayers when in the few days following the verdict I began to find peace of mind.

Having established acceptance over the cause of death it still remained within me to work through the process of bereavement. It had never occurred to me that the pain of losing someone could be almost more severe a year later. I had been used to going for long periods of time without seeing Kathie; often our only means of keeping up to date with one another was by post. So a year of not having seen her didn't feel strange, but subconsciously I always lived in hope that a letter would arrive. In fact it was not until three years after she had died, that on the anniversary of her death I could think of her and remember the good times we had without the terrible stabbing pain.

An essential part of the bereavement process was for me to return to Bermuda where Kathie had spent virtually all her working life. I had been out there to stay with her on two occasions and if I were to achieve complete acceptance it meant a third visit to the isolated island in the vast Atlantic Ocean. Sixteen months after Kathie had died, friends of hers in Bermuda wrote and asked if I would like to come and stay. I accepted the invitation and asked if my sister, Ruth, might join me.

We boarded the plane and it soared up into the cloud-filled sky. Six hours later we caught our first glimpse of the rich turquoise sea surrounding Bermuda. For me it brought about happy memories and for Ruth it stimulated excitement at her first visit to the Fairy-tale Island.

Joy was at the airport to meet us; she and her husband, Peter, had been like substitute parents to Kathie, who had moved to Bermuda shortly after finishing at art school and soon after her mother had died. I knew Peter and Joy well.

We climbed into the car. The island certainly held an air of intrigue; there was something almost intangible about it. Being back amongst its sub-tropical beauty and dense vegetation was probably the most exhilarating experience I had had recently. Exhilarating, because one cannot go to an island such as Bermuda and not be swept into a realm of excitement and mystery, and yet I cannot say that the three weeks were altogether enjoyable. For a complete healing to take place it meant that the wound which through the passage of time had closed to form a faint scar would have to be opened again in order that any remaining poison be removed.

Naturally, people on the island wanted to talk about Kathie's death and their confusion and anger over what had happened. They wanted to talk about the mysteries; even question the coroner's report. Several felt sure that it was murder and had reason for saying so. The effect that this had on me was to steal away the acceptance I had more recently found.

Night after night I cried out to God, 'Lord, why must I go through this; how long must I endure such agony?' God held in his hands a beautiful tapestry; the Creator was at work. But I was standing on the reverse side; all I could see was a mess, a conglomeration of knots and stray ends. Slowly the Lord was to reveal to me His work of art; a picture which spoke of the depths of His comfort and the enrichment of life.

When the pain was at its worst I felt a deep need to express suppressed emotions and talk with someone who would not just write off my feelings. The Lord graciously answered my prayer, though it was little more than a pitiful cry, when a few hours later Ann called round. She had been a close friend of Kathie's and I had met her on my previous visits. We drove out to Stonington Beach Hotel where we sat and talked over a couple of large iced cokes. The sea beat rhythmically in the distance and the sinking sun cast a golden path on its crystal surface. How could anyone doubt the existence of the Creator? How could anyone doubt that Kathie, who was a committed Christian, had walked along that golden path into the rays of immortality and now stood in the brilliant light of the Son?

For the first time I saw a glimmer of hope. Those few hours had been full of pain and yet were very beautiful. I knew that Ann understood, because it was her loss too and in the empathy we had for one another there was great security to be found.

As I returned to the house I had a picture of the Lord's hand reaching down into my bottomless pit and calling me to take hold and allow Him to pull me out.

A few days later our plane soared into the midnight air leaving behind the silhouette of a scorpion-shaped island covered in a mass of little dots of light. Bermuda was gone and there lay ahead at least six hours of Atlantic Ocean.

In the early hours of the morning, when most people were fast asleep, I opened the Easter card that Ann had given me. Inside was a letter that spoke from the bottom of her heart.

At the present time of 2.00 a.m. I am wide awake thinking of you and Kathie. I do hope that our talk has not upset you too much or opened up wounds that were better left alone.

Kathie's death has bothered me a lot as I felt I had no-one I could discuss it with. You and I must both believe she is happy now and that she does live and we *will* see her again. That really is the basis of Christianity as I perceive it.

There was great comfort and truth in Ann's words and in the light of what she had said, the ability to 'let go' finally came.

3

Love for evermore

Take from my heart
this pain of mine
and plant your seed
of love divine.

Take from my eyes
these tears which flow
and let my faith
now ever grow.

Take from my mind
this sense of loss
and help me place
it at the cross.

Take from my body
my hopelessness
and hold me in
your arms for rest.

Then teach me death's
not a closed door
that there's love now
and for evermore.

The Lord had taken my pain, my tears, my sense of loss, my hopelessness, and was graciously teaching me that death is not a closed door.

The effect of losing someone so close by so untimely and mysterious a death could have been enough to send me back into the throes of anorexia which I had only been free of for a couple of years, or even to have shaken my newly-found faith. But, instead, the Lord planted His seed of love divine and used the experience to draw me ever closer to Him.

At the back of my mind I had always had a picture of death as something gruesome and to be feared. A sudden darkness that drops from the sky like a black blanket, come to smother and extinguish the fire of life; a howling gale which sweeps through every nation turning warm, happy people into cold, emotionless corpses. No respecter of age, circumstance or wealth, it comes to steal children and adults, rich and poor alike, leaving behind its shadow of emptiness, pain and turmoil.

I had no knowledge of what death is, only experience of the void that it leaves behind. After Kathie had died and I had finally accepted the fact that she was no longer around, the Lord took me through a process of discovery. For months after Kathie's death every time I saw someone who looked vaguely like her I would follow them from street to street, shop to shop, believing that she had for some reason changed her identity and would turn round, notice me and confess.

What seemed to me to be totally unacceptable was the harshness and finality that death brought with it. But as the Lord led me into the process of discovery I began to realise that 'harshness' and 'finality' are two very inappropriate words for the committed Christian. Firstly the Lord had to teach me what death is and He did this at a totally unexpected moment when I was curious to know more of what the book of Revelation contains.

So I looked, and behold, an ashy pale horse (black and blue as if made so by bruising) and its rider's name was Death, and Hades (the realm of the dead) followed him closely; and they were given authority and power over a fourth part of the earth, to kill with the sword and with famine and with plague (pestilence, disease) and with wild beasts of the earth.
(Revelation 6:8, The Amplified Bible)

Then I saw a great white throne and the One Who was seated upon it, from Whose presence and from the sight of Whose face earth and sky fled away and no place was found for them.

I (also) saw the dead, great and small; they stood before the throne, and books were opened. Then another book was opened, which is (the Book) of Life. And the dead were judged (sentenced) by what they had done (their whole way of feeling and acting, their aims and endeavours) in accordance with what was recorded in the books.

And the sea delivered up the dead who were in it, Death and Hades (the state of death or disembodied existence) surrendered the dead in them; and all were tried and their cases determined by what they had done – according to their motives, aims and works.

Then Death and Hades (the state of death or disembodied existence) were thrown into the lake of fire. This is the second death, the lake of fire.

> *And if any one's (name) was not found recorded in the
> Book of Life, he was hurled into the lake of fire.*
> (Revelation 20:11-15, The Amplified Bible)

So, death is a person, a satanic being. It helped to see it in
such a way; to 'identify' death, and it was comforting to
know that in the Final Judgement death will be destroyed
forever, so that when the New Heaven and the New Earth
come *there will be no more death, no more grief or crying or pain*
(Revelation 21:4, GNB).

How fantastic! I thought. But that is *after* the Final
Judgement; what about now whilst death still roams the
earth? After all it is the only certainty for everyone alive
– no one can escape and all must submit – one day each
and every one of us will be faced with death. Does that
mean that we too will come face to face with the rider on
the ashy pale horse and be swept into his evil clutches?

Slowly my eyes were being opened. Why, apart from
to teach us many things, did Jesus come down to earth?
To pay the price of sin and therefore reconcile us to
God. The wages of sin is death, and so Jesus' mission
was to defeat death. He suffered the intense agony
which should have been ours – separation from God
the Father. So gruesome was His suffering to be that
whilst in the garden of Gethsemane He cried out to
God, *My Father, if it is possible, take this cup of suffering
from me! Yet not what I want, but what you want* (Matthew
26:39, GNB). Then as He hung dying, bleeding and
gaunt, He cried out, *It is finished* (John 19:30, GNB). The
price had been paid.

Death had finally lost its sting, and those who have
trusted in Jesus as their Saviour will experience Him as
their Victor at the time of their 'dying'. For them, 'death'
is an inapplicable word. There will be no 'death'; there
will be no rider on the ashy pale horse. For their dying
came when, in accepting to follow Jesus, they died to self
and were born again in Christ. At their 'end' they will

merely pass from the restrictions of life on earth to the freedom of life in eternity.

> *Our brothers, we want you to know the truth about those who have died, so that you will not be sad, as are those who have no hope. We believe that Jesus died and rose again and so we believe that God will take back with Jesus those who have died believing in him* (1 Thessalonians 4:13-14, GNB).

I found the concept of a mortal body and an immortal soul very difficult to grasp, probably due to the fact that my mind works on a pictorial (artistic) wave-length as opposed to an intellectual one. Then when my grand-mother died a year or two after Kathie, insight into this concept was finally given. For the first time I looked upon the body of a dead person and what struck me above all else was that what lay before my eyes was merely a shell. I could feel the emptiness; it was as empty as the outer layer of a chrysalis is after the newly-created butterfly has emerged. This shell was not my grandmother; my grand-mother was the strong, courageous, determined char-acter I had come to know, love and appreciate. And it was this that lived on. At the same time the Lord gave me another beautiful insight – a glimpse of Heaven through a dream. I dreamt that my grandmother phoned me up. I was amazed to hear her voice, she was calling from Heaven! All she wanted to know was how I was; all I wanted to know was how she was! She told me she was with grandad again and she sounded delighted.

'But are you happy, Gran?' I asked.

'Happy?' She sounded hesitant, almost as if she didn't understand.

'Yes, happy.' I repeated.

Then suddenly I realised that I was speaking a different 'language'. 'Happy' was something that belonged to Earth; the equivalent in Heaven was a feeling ten times greater than ecstasy.

'Yes, I'm happy,' she said, and I could sense the smile in her voice as if she was saying, 'One day my child you'll know what true "happiness" is.'

If I had learnt one thing over the months it was to value life. I began to see how easy it is to waste the years that we are given. To live idly, each day the same as the day before and equally as mundane. To sit in front of the television and watch life slip away. To procrastinate and put off doing for others those things which often cost us time and effort. Life passed too quickly not to work for goals and to see those goals fulfilled.

Life started to take on a sense of urgency, as if I should be living as though each day were my last – for no one knows when death will call! Every morning I made the decision to spend the next twelve hours in such a way that I would not regret my actions. It seemed a pretty idealistic way to live and I wondered whether I was becoming too much of a deep thinker and everyone would consider me some kind of mad and impractical philosopher. Then reading the psalms one day I noticed that the psalmist also had the same thoughts.

> *Teach us how short our life is*
> *so that we may become wise.*
> (Psalm 90:12, GNB)

> *You carry us away like a flood;*
> *we last no longer than a dream.*
> *We are like weeds that sprout in the morning,*
> *that grow and burst into bloom,*
> *then dry up and die in the evening.*
> (Psalm 90:5-6, GNB)

What did living each day as if it were my last mean? It meant that I would always keep my eyes on Jesus. That I would remember Him throughout the day, have time to read the Bible and pray, not turn away those in need because I was too tired, fed up or did not have time for them. In all, it meant living in such a way that if I were called to Heaven or Jesus returned I would not have to say, 'Why do you come to take me now? I'm not ready yet!'

I don't believe that God calls us to live in perfection, but as the psalmist says, it is good to number our days so that we may become wise; to live with wisdom and not with a constant stream of regrets. Too often death comes as a thief in the night when we are least expecting it. Our days here on Earth are short compared to life in eternity; as small as a teardrop is to all the water in the oceans. I consider that the years we are given in these mortal bodies are in preparation for eternity; that life is a lesson, a time of learning, growth and getting ready. Yet most of us spend our time making provisions for this life, disregarding the next, because we cannot face up to the fact that death is a reality.

We make provisions for so-called 'security' and 'comfort' – well-furnished houses, central heating, televisions and dvds (with remote control of course!) cars, hi-fi and the latest technology in labour-saving devices. We make provision for the future, money in the bank, building society, investment schemes and interest. A little stacked away for a rainy day, and if we are fortunate a little to take a trip to the tropical sun; and if we're unfortunate a little to pay for the false teeth, hearing aids, glasses, wigs and wooden legs when we're over the hill! There is much need for money, comfort and security and I am not decrying them, except where they are at the expense of making provision for the life to come. After all, from dust we came and to dust we shall return (without all our belongings!).

We are confronted with death all the time. We only have to turn on the television or radio to hear of yet more tragedies around the world – war, chaos, earthquakes, fires and car crashes. Such 'tragedies' can have the beneficial effect of shaking us out of our complacency towards sin and becoming 'worldly'. It certainly shook me out of my complacency towards both of these things, giving life a quality that I had not experienced before. It also implanted within me a desire to reach out to other people; to draw them closer to God, to help them know the beautiful peace, love and joy that can be theirs through opening their lives to Him. And to enable them to get life into perspective; to think in terms of eternity.

I had not thought much about Heaven and Hell before; they always sounded to me like places out of a fairy tale – 'those who do good will live happily ever after in paradise and those who do evil will perish in the fires below!' Then one day I heard someone speak of why he started to look into Christianity and consequently became converted – he was terrified of ending up in Hell. Not long after hearing his testimony I read the account of a doctor who had a very similar experience. A patient came into his consulting room and whilst there suffered a heart attack; the doctor immediately started resuscitation, and as the patient came round he was shouting about being in the horrors of Hell. The reality of the patient's description hit the doctor hard and gave him a hunger to find out exactly what Heaven and Hell were all about; in the process of delving into the Bible he became a Christian!

These two incidents set me thinking; if God can only accept into His kingdom those who have allowed Jesus into their lives – as is Biblical, *No one goes to the Father except by me* (John 14:6, GNB) – and if all others will eventually be thrown into the Lake of Fire, it is a very sad thing. To think of those we love ending in this way and being separated from us for evermore is enough to shake us into acting on Jesus' command, *Go then to all people everywhere and make them my disciples: baptise them in the name of the Father, the Son and the Holy Spirit and teach them to obey everything I have commanded you. And I will be with you always, until the end of the age'* (Matthew 28:19-20, GNB).

In all that Jesus suffered for us we have an obligation to tell others of the options they have, to try to help them find the narrow path; to teach them the reality of both Heaven *and* Hell and think twice about living life without the Lord.

Having a burning desire to tell others about the reality of Heaven and Hell and to help them reach a stage of commitment was all very well, but I still found it very difficult to believe that I *personally* would make it to Heaven. I suppose feelings of inferiority and failure which had been implanted within me from childhood were as good a reason as any for believing that all the Christians I had spoken with would make it except me! Whenever I heard people proclaim that they are 'saved' and 'have a one way ticket to Heaven' it always sounded very pious. I couldn't bring myself to say such a thing for fear that the joke might be on me one day! It was only more recently whilst at a Hospital Christian Fellowship conference in South Africa that I was finally able to grasp that accepting Jesus into one's life means having salvation and that in turn salvation ensures eternal life (going to Heaven). That it is by *God's grace* and *not* by our *own efforts* that we shall participate in this, and therefore there is nothing pious about proclaiming it.

Soon after I arrived I heard Gerry Landry speak of his brief encounter with death. Apart from his beautiful description of Heaven in all its tranquillity, the one thing that really spoke to me was his parting message: 'Having been there and back, I can tell you with certainty that death holds no fear for those who have been saved by the blood of Jesus.' Here was a man who had seen the reality of life after death as a Christian and spoke of beauty, peace, awe and wonder. If this should be his experience why should it not be mine?

I felt moved and challenged by Gerry's words and

started to feel a little more confident that I might just make it to Heaven by the skin of my teeth! But still underneath lay that niggling feeling that one day I might also be in for a terrible shock.

Then came the wonderful follow-up. I found myself sharing a room with one of the HCF workers, and for some reason Erica and I got onto the subject of salvation. Immediately I expressed my difficulty in believing that I am saved, she showed me a verse in the Bible, *I am writing this to you so that you may know that you have eternal life – you that believe in the Son of God* (1 John 5:13, GNB). As I read the verse, it suddenly dawned on me that I had not really looked at what the Bible had to say but had been too fond of reading what everyone else had written on the subject. Erica pointed out the importance of always looking to the Bible for the answer. The passage did not say we can *hope* we have eternal life, but we can *know* we have eternal life.

She explained that eternal life came naturally with accepting Jesus. That by God's grace we shall live in union with the Son and the Father forever. By the time I was due to leave the conference I had no doubts whatsoever that one day I will taste the delights of Heaven, and what a beautiful day that will be! No more hardship or suffering. No more tears. Then I shall be living in a land of perfect love and unity.

When I arrived back home the Lord gave me confirmation after confirmation that I am saved. Every time I opened the Bible for the next few days I discovered yet another passage proclaiming eternal life. The Lord was not going to let me forget that one day I will meet with Him in Heaven. Nor was I going to forget the promise that He had given me.

If you confess that Jesus is Lord and believe that God raised him from death, you will be saved. For it is by our faith that we are put right with God; it is by our confession that we are saved. The scripture says, 'Whoever believes in him will not be disappointed' (Romans 10:9-11, GNB).

Be sure then to keep in your hearts the message you heard from the beginning. If you keep that message, then you will always live in union with the Son and the Father. And this is what Christ himself promised to give us – eternal life (1 John 2:24-25, GNB).

4

Conflict

What is love if it means
Tearing each other apart;
Destroying my confidence,
Breaking your heart?

What is love if it means
Shattered communication;
Pain and resentment,
A fading relation?

How if there's love within
Can we put the past between,
Hold onto our guilt
And hide what we've seen?

How if there's love within
Can we still not share;
Sorrow and regrets
With each other bear?

Why if there's love
Is conflict a must,
Setting barriers between
And a lack of trust?

Why if there's love
Can't we feel free;
Our independence value,
Our difference let be?

Bereavement had brought with it an empty hole and only one month after Kathie's death I found myself in the throes of engagement as a subconscious effort to fill the void. It was a fairy-tale romance that began the day before Christmas Eve with brass bands playing in the streets, cheering up the cold, damp weather as we wandered around the shops looking for a ring, and then the excitement of waking up on Christmas morning to announce that Andy and I were now engaged – I was nineteen.

I had known Andy since I was eleven when we had met at a summer drama school. I was sitting on a darkened stage, cross-legged, contemplating with my eyes closed, when suddenly my body went into a hot sweat – Andy had turned the spotlights on me! The occasional 'I love you' note followed and a few years later, a song about me materialised. It was inevitable that, despite our comings and goings, the relationship would deepen.

What arose was the ecstatic feeling of falling in love; of knowing that someone cared enough to want to spend the rest of their life with me. The feeling was good; almost addictive. I rose to the heights of joy and walked around with stars in my eyes. It was nice to feel needed, special, chosen, and it was nice to give. Pain seemed easier to bear as well, all I had to do was to cover it in a veneer of this love that I had found and no one would be any the wiser as to what really lay underneath. If

I painted it thick enough I could even fool myself!

What I did not realise was that whilst Andy and I were able to share many good moments together, in fact I had been bowled over by an emotion rather than fallen in love with a person. As the novelty of being engaged wore off and the excitement died down, I saw that underneath lay two incompatible people, very different in nature, ideas, interests and emotional make-up; suited on a friendship basis, but not for marriage. I too was far from ready or capable of a marriage relationship. Each day our differences showed that little bit more and the friction increased to such an extent that I was at breaking point. I knew that the relationship had to come to an end, but felt guilty that I was the one who seemed to be causing it to break up. It appeared that Andy still loved me dearly and that in his eyes there was nothing wrong with our relationship. But I had to be true to myself and to him.

Everyone else around had been capable of seeing the mistake I was making but 'love' had blinded me and I walked into the situation devoid of any light. Underneath I knew how other people felt, but refused to hear what they were saying for fear that they would openly reject the idea. They were thinking in terms of marriage – I was (subconsciously) thinking of an immediate pain reliever and filler of the void. What hurt me most about my actions was that I had not once prayed about the engagement or put it in God's hands. I had selfishly set out to resolve my problems, pain and confusion alone.

Now Andy was gone, leaving a bunch of flowers and a note saying I was free to do what I wanted. At last the pressure was off me, as Andy said, I was 'free'. Yet I felt desperately confused and hurt and anything but free. Where tension and frustration lay before, emptiness and loneliness stepped in.

Days later I had reached a point beyond helping myself. I thought that going to church in the evening and being amongst Christian friends, God would be bound to melt and remould me. What I desired was an instant emotional cure without having to put any effort in myself or even acknowledge that the Lord was the healer. It didn't happen! I could not have felt more alone if I had been on a deserted island. My self-pity had got such a hold that I was screaming blue murder at myself, yet refusing to let God help me.

I realised the situation had to be resolved from the minute I set foot in the Crossroads (young people's) meeting after church.

Despite my unease I made a conscious decision to stay in the meeting. Then Andy came and sat next to me and I felt the muscles in my stomach knot up. When we started to sing I couldn't hit any of the notes and I knew that I most definitely couldn't pray. My thoughts were not on God, they were on one long escape. Escape from people, feelings and circumstances.

At last the opportunity to make a subtle exit from the meeting arose. I saw no point in being a dormant hypocrite – sitting, singing and saying words that I did not mean. I needed to get myself right with the Lord.

The rain lashed down as I marched on towards the station. I was going home. Come lightning or thunder or the earth cracking beneath my feet, nothing was going to stop me. A few drunks wandered past. 'So what! At least they can laugh,' I said enviously. I hit the lamp post beside me hard. The jolt must have shaken some sense into my grey matter as I cried out to God for help, 'God, I can't run away from the situation, but nor can I help myself, you've got to do something, you've got to help me.' Slowly I walked back to the church and leant against the wall outside.

My feelings of love for God were very great but the negative emotions which continued to crowd my mind made the distance between God and myself feel enormous. Past scars had been re-opened and were bleeding.

I hurt so much and I knew that God was the only one who could help me, yet something was preventing me from allowing Him to work.

I turned my head to one side. Andy was standing close by.

'Can I help?' he said kindly.

Remaining motionless I mumbled, 'I'm afraid only God can help.'

He disappeared before I could blink twice. Then I heard footsteps coming from the other side. It had to be Joan. I felt a sudden panic flood my body and wondered what to do. Two thoughts entered my mind simultaneously – either I run as fast as my legs will take me, because she's bound to hit the nail on the head and I can't face reality, or else I give in and try to talk. My mind longed to take the first option but my legs refused to co-operate!

Although lack of sleep had brought about an inability to concentrate, not all of what Joan said went in one ear and out of the other; a couple of points had an impact on me. One was the way I had set myself unrealistically high standards and in falling short of those standards I walked straight into self-condemnation. I condemned myself both for being the one to break off the engagement, and for acting within the engagement in a way that was not pleasing to God. I had totally ignored the fact that in Christ there is *no* condemnation, and that God desires to work through bad or difficult situations for our good. Condemning myself only built up barriers between God and me. I was saying to God, 'Don't bother to call me, I'll call you, because I'm just not worth looking at at the moment.'

This tied in with Joan's second point which was that effectively I had taken my hand out of the clasp of God's hand and was trying to do everything in my own strength instead of paying heed to what Jesus said, *Come to me, all of you who are tired from carrying heavy loads, and I will give you rest* (Matthew 11:28, GNB).

To put it bluntly I was being stubborn; and seeking to find the answers in the world and other people resulted in one bad day drifting into another. Only seconds after my eyes had opened clouds of darkness hung oppressively above my head. The thought of getting up to face another day was too daunting.

The crunch came one day soon after I had forced myself out of bed and down the stairs. The ever-increasing clouds were joined by a sack of guilt, lying unbearably upon my already breaking back. Guilt over everything I could possibly find to feel guilty about! For being loved and not showing love back. For promising to love and serve God, then not even finding time to pray with Him. For accepting Jesus as my personal Saviour but responding as if I hardly knew Him.

As I lethargically ambled into the kitchen and put the kettle on, one question and cry to God ran continuously through my mind. 'How can you still take me as your child if I fail you every time?' The kettle boiled, the post shot through the letter-box and the cat demanded to be fed with a piercing meow. Still I stood motionless. I felt so useless, an utter failure; I couldn't even live up to the person God intended me to be. I was even beginning to feel guilty that in a few minutes I would be asking God yet again to forgive my sins; perhaps because I always seem to commit the same sort of sins, and am fully aware that although God offers us complete forgiveness of all sins, He does expect us to turn from them.

I stared out of the kitchen window at the myriad of newly-formed spring flowers, each perfect in its formation, and related the picture to the emotions which were flooding my body, negative emotions which proved to be unlike the delicacy and beauty of the spring flowers. They were fully destructive, equalling that of a frost, come to ruin God's work of art in creation. I longed to release myself from such emotions but all efforts to do so failed. Determined not to be defeated, I temporarily washed away the bad feelings with a much-needed cup of coffee, and drowned the remainder in a bath.

My few minutes of relaxation came to an abrupt end, as I stepped out of the bath to face reality; reality that I couldn't cope with the burdens resting heavily upon my shoulders. I covered up my feelings until everyone had left the house. I even tried convincing myself that there was nothing wrong, but soon came to the conclusion that whilst I might be able to fool others, I couldn't fool myself! My thoughts turned to work; I couldn't even face going there in a couple of hours. 'What now God?' I cried and broke down. There was no one to support me; any support had to come from God alone.

I poured my woes upon Him and reached out like a helpless child in need of being picked up and loved. He felt very close; but instead of just feeling a deep sense of love and peace, I was conscious of God telling me to stop snivelling and fetch my Bible. He then went on to speak to me through particular passages in an amazing way.

Whilst pouring out my woes, I had asked Him several questions –

- Will I go on feeling humiliated, distressed and lonely?
- Can you still love me when I fail you and can you truly forgive my sins?
- How will I receive strength to cope with life?
- What do you want me to do in the future and what kind of person do you expect me to be?

In the passages I read, God answered all my questions. Firstly I turned to 2 Corinthians 1:8-10. After reading it through a couple of times I wrote down what I felt God was saying to me:

The problems which you have had have been very great and I know that at times you have felt like giving up all hope, even to the extent of giving up living. But the reason I have allowed this to happen is to teach you that you must rely not on yourself, but only on me. I have helped you through difficult times and will continue to do so if you place your hope in me.

From 2 Corinthians I turned to Isaiah 61 and 62 where again I sat quietly and listened to what God was saying to me:

Don't be afraid – you will not be disgraced again, nor humiliated. You will forget your unfaithfulness and your desperate loneliness; I, your creator, will take care of you. I will save you.

For one moment you might have felt as though I had deserted you. Now I call you back to me with deep love; a love that I will show you for evermore. Worldly goods may vanish, human love may fall away, but my love for you can never end.

I know that you are suffering, that you feel helpless with no one to comfort you. Come to me. I want to rebuild your life into something precious. I want to show you that you will have prosperity and peace; to teach you that justice and right will make you strong and to tell you that you will be safe from fear and oppression.

I shall speak out to encourage you, Helena, and I shall perform many good works in you. I will not be quiet until you are restored and until you are saved.

You will have a new name, a name given by myself. You will no longer be known as 'forsaken' but you will be called 'God is pleased with you'. Because I am pleased with you, your life will no longer be known as 'deserted' but 'happily married'. Whether I give you a husband or whether you remain with the one who formed you, you will be happy and I will take delight in you.

I have filled you with my Spirit. I have chosen you to help those in need, the poor, the broken-hearted and those who have done wrong. I have sent you to proclaim my word; to sow joy and praise where sorrow and grief have been planted. I myself will sow these new seeds through you, and you will praise me.

I did praise Him because he had spoken to me in the most amazing way. My thoughts, emotions and attitudes were beginning to change. Even so, the negative effects of my broken engagement were a compulsive desire to retreat into myself. In feeling hurt through losing love, though it was my choice, I had to watch that the temptation to isolate myself did not force me into the 'bottomless pit'.

So often in a crisis situation, we have a choice either to come away wounded and broken, or to allow God to use the experience for our good. Despite the pain I went through, I did not once regret my walking into the engagement, or later, my decision to break it off because of the lessons I had learned.

If there was one thing I felt God taught me through these months it was about love; the meaning and depth of love and how the love of God is necessary for our relationship with one another.

I saw that love is much more than an infatuation, physical attraction or merely an emotion. It is the most important and powerful thing in existence because God is love – it is the foundation of all else and without it everything is useless.

I may be able to speak the languages of men and even of angels, but if I have no love, my speech is no more than a noisy gong or clanging bell. I may have the gift of inspired preaching; I may have all knowledge and understand all secrets; I may have all the faith to move mountains – but if I have no love, I am nothing (1 Corinthians 13:1-2, GNB).

It is by this love that we shall be recognised as Jesus' disciples. Such love is patient and kind; it is not jealous or envious, conceited or proud. It is not rude, selfish, short-tempered or irritable. Nor does it keep a record of wrongs; it is all forgiving. It is not happy with evil, only with truth (Own adaptation of 1 Corinthians 13:4-6).

A purely human love (without God) could never have all these qualities.

Love is eternal, immortal. All else will come to an end. Even faith and hope, there will be no need for these in heaven, but there will always be a need for love. Therefore it is love that we should set our hearts and minds on; it is love for which we should strive.

I saw too the scale of love – gentle, tender and caring, great and powerful.

To be secure in further relationships I felt that it was vital to comprehend the extent of God's love for me. Without the knowledge and security of God's great love I knew that I could not stand up to human love falling away or to being rebuffed or rejected in the future. Being confident in God's love for me is also the only way I have been able to cope with the desperate moments of loneliness brought about through being single and as a result of other issues in my life.

Such times have taught me that it is the quality and not the quantity of love that is of importance. As I have surrendered the aspects of life that I find difficult to God, so He has revealed to me more and more of His love, which proves to be an endless source of comfort and strength. In addition I see more of just how much God is in control of our lives and holds our futures securely in His hands, that He lays down paths for us to walk along and that, though we may stumble and fall, He does not allow us to be tested beyond our ability to remain firm.

5

Tramps and TV interviews

Tramps and TV interviews,
a damp London Station
and piles of book reviews.

My first book
on the shelf
No – not instant wealth!

Life full of contrast;
each day a play
with a new cast.

Microphones and studios,
what's in the future?
Well, who knows!

I was relieved that the trauma of the broken engagement was over several months before the publication of my first book, *Puppet on a String*, was due and I could concentrate fully on what would probably prove to be one of the most exciting days of my life.

The build-up to the publication of the book had not been at all as I had expected. Only a month before *Puppet on a String* was due to be put on the market I was called to the publishers to discuss publicity. As I walked into the office I was confronted by a large poster of myself, and someone said in jest, 'Have you got one of these?' handing me a copy of the book.

'No, I haven't actually!' I answered, stretching out my hand to receive it. A great surge of joy broke forth; it seemed incredible that the pile of handwritten notes which increased daily in order to purge deep emotions out of my system was now a complete book, almost ready for the market. But as I held the book in my hand and stared at it my feelings became more and more negative and I began to regret ever having written it. It was as though speaking of my own experience with anorexia, revealing past pain and baring my soul was to create a crushing vulnerability. Emotions as deep as fear and hatred started to arise and I wanted to lash out and destroy every copy of the book that had been printed. I never dreamt that joy and excitement would be replaced by such negativity and it felt as though on the day of publication I was to be dragged out into the street, stripped naked and shot publicly!

God understood completely my utter vulnerability and caught me up in His arms, reminding me of how much he had been with me thus far and His goodness in providing me with the loveliest of literary agents and a first-time acceptance by one of the best publishers – Hodder and Stoughton. God had a purpose in the publication of this book and only if I were prepared to give of myself could it touch the hearts and lives of others. But He would be my shield and my protector and tuck me safely under the shadow of His wing whenever the wind blew.

By the day of publication all negative emotion had been swept away and enthusiasm restored to its fullest. I woke up in the morning realising that never again would I experience the feeling of sheer exhilaration at having a first book published, and an unspeakable joy flowed through my every vein. I began to see a purpose in the suffering of my teens, how God had worked through it for good, and I was filled with a deep love. A love that was not stagnant but would manifest itself in action and give me the courage and strength to face the many interviews and talks which lay ahead.

Radio and television interviews of which I had lived in fear for weeks proved to be a constant source of amusement and after about the fifth interview I actually looked forward to my half-hour or so of studio existence and deep conversation with a microphone! Radio interviews took me around the country from London to Newcastle and even sent my voice over the air to Belfast whilst sitting in Radio Oxford clutching a pair of bright red, over-sized headphones to my ears in an attempt to understand an Irish accent saying,

'Oxford, can you hear me? Go ahead Oxford.'

To think that I would get away with only straightforward interviews was a mistake. Only about the second time I had been on air I was asked to participate in a programme called 'A month in a monastery', where through the art of imagination I had to picture how I would spend a month alone, what my choice of music and literature for that time would be and how I would fare emotionally and spiritually.

The first television interview turned into a day of entertainment, when the crew came down to my parents' home, and seeing what a beautiful garden we had, decided it would be nice to film outside. It was a pleasantly sunny April day but cold to be sitting outside in a cotton blouse for long, and as the minutes ticked on I lost all sensation in my feet and desperately hoped that my teeth didn't start chattering. Little did the viewers know that the chair on which I was seated had been placed on somewhat unstable ground and if I were to do as much as uncross my legs or twist my head I ran the risk of doing a very unladylike backward somersault into the pond behind me!

Public speaking was not something I welcomed with open arms. I cannot deny that my whole body shook with fear on the first few occasions of having to stand up before a crowd of mature adults and talk for forty-five minutes, when I myself had only just made it into adulthood and still very much felt like a child. As with the radio interviews, experience calmed the nerves and created a healthy amount of self-confidence and after about six months I was able to say that I actually quite enjoyed myself. I remember the first time I was asked to speak, and how to begin with I was completely dumbfounded as all I was aware of were row upon row of eyes focused on me. I opened my mouth and somehow words poured out, but as time progressed, to my absolute horror I realised that my carefully prepared notes were on the far side of the table and to get to them meant clambering over tangled microphone wires which seemed to have congregated around my feet! I decided to abandon the idea of notes and carried on ad-libbing. When at the end a loud applause materialised I decided that if I had coped the first time without notes, the second time with notes would be a giveaway!

After I had delivered my talk people were invited to ask questions. The subject matter of eating disorders had aroused such deep interest that questions came as an endless stream. After a great length of time the person who had invited me to speak noticed that I was flagging and put an end to the questions, saying that I would be available to sign copies of my book and talk personally with anyone who felt the need. People came in their dozens and I realised from that very first talk that such occasions were going to involve a complete giving of myself. I sat listening to and holding the hand of a woman whose daughter had died of anorexia only a few months previously. She spoke of the pain that her daughter had endured, of the ferocity of the battle inside her body and mind, the will to live and then suddenly the loss of it.

At the end of every talk I gave, I received from those present nothing other than praise for my willingness to share so openly and expose the depths of pain. It was thankful hearts such as these that gave me the strength to cope with any criticism from the media which came my way. I was fortunate that, in the thirty or so news-paper and magazine articles that came out in the weeks following the publication of the book, only two con-tained harsh words, one even having the audacity to say that I was not completely through the experience, that I used religion to half-recover and that the book contained an element of smugness about it – desperately worrying if read by other anorexics.

If I could first get over the pain of having a very personal piece of writing attacked, the criticism actually proved quite laughable. This was especially so when this 'dangerous to be read by other sufferers' book resulted in hundreds of letters on the doormat from hurting people who had found my words a source of strength and encouragement!

As I found myself becoming more and more involved in the lives of hurting people, and seeking to respond to the cries for help that flooded in, I realised that through the publication of *Puppet on a String* God's revelation for my life (that He had chosen me to 'help those in need, the poor, the broken-hearted and those who have done wrong') was happening! It was very subtle; I had been actively involved in listening to the pain-filled words of people caught in the grip of anorexia and depression for several months before it actually dawned on me that this was the work to which God had already assigned me.

Similarly I had found myself spending time amongst the down-and-outs in the dark and dank parts of London, and starting to fulfil another part of God's revelation for my life in seeking to help the poor, or at least show my compassion for them.

My first encounter with such people was on a winter's evening. The London sky was dark and oppressive, rain fell in heavy sheets and I shivered in the damp. It was a relief to reach the shelter of the railway station. I had two hours before my train departed and as all the seats on the station were taken I found a place on the floor outside a bookstall, pulled out a note pad from my bag and started writing. It hardly seemed the place to be creating an article but since I was feeling inspired and had time on my hands the surroundings faded into insignificance.

My battle with words came to an abrupt halt when it was interrupted by a coarse cockney voice.

'Lidy, Lidy.'

I looked up to see a beggar woman, pale-faced; her mousy hair tangled and dirty; her skin coated in London's filth and her clothing shabby and over-sized.

Hesitantly I leant forward; her breath smelt strongly of alcohol, her teeth were black and decayed. She mumbled something about being hungry and thirsty and shoved a pile of grubby change into my hands. She had been kicked out of the shop; they didn't want people like her in a half-drunken stupor being a nuisance. I felt sorry for her and did as she had asked.

'Thank you lidy, thank you. My 'usband said you'd run off with the money, but I said you wouldn'.'

I smiled and sat down, making a clear decision not to become involved.

The woman opened the bottle of drink, took several mouthfuls and placed herself next to me, dragging her reluctant husband by the arm. Angry words flew in every direction and I turned a blind eye to their aggressive mannerisms.

'Young lidy, would ya like some?' the woman asked as she waved the bottle under my nose.

'No thanks,' I replied, hastily unwrapping some chocolate so as not to feel awkward.

'Shut up will ya,' the woman snapped back at her husband who was still complaining bitterly about having to sit down, 'I'm talkin' to the nice young lidy.'

She turned in my direction and suddenly all my pride melted away and I passed through the mirror of life to experience the reflection of another's existence.

'What ya studying, young lidy?' the woman asked.

'Oh! I'm just writing,' was my non-committal answer.

'You're a very kind person,' she continued. 'Ya know there are some evil people in this world, very evil: see that woman over there?'

She pointed to a thin figure whose sunken black eyes contrasted with a deathly white face.

'She's one of 'em.'

At that moment the other woman staggered in our direction, quite obviously intoxicated with alcohol. As she drew closer I noticed her very drawn and lined face;

it should have belonged to someone thirty years her senior and was a pitiful sight. She forced her way between us and the two women sat and talked, but I sensed a feeling of hatred between them.

Within seconds the shadowy figure disappeared into the background and the woman turned to me again.

'She's a troublemaker. See this scar?' She pointed to a deep line across her face. 'She done that to me. You wanna stay away from 'er.'

She turned to her husband and started arguing furiously with him because he was beckoning the woman over again. It seemed that they were both troublemakers and that the woman next to me was fighting their evil force.

She slipped her hand into her coat pocket and pulled out a slender bottle of perfume.

'Go on, try it,' she urged.

I dabbed a little on my wrists. The sweet fragrance was welcome after the less pleasant smell of unwashed bodies.

'Keep it,' she said.

'No, it's all right, you have it,' I replied, knowing full well that it was about her only possession.

'It's only wasted on me and I'd like you to have it for bein' kind,' she said.

I was deeply touched by her generosity.

Her husband clearly saw this as an ideal opportunity for taking money.

'You ain't takin' no money off 'er', the woman retorted, 'she's only a poor student; there's much richer people than 'er around 'ere.'

I looked up at the stream of affluent people walking past, businessmen in their well-pressed suits, women in the latest fashions. Each person was alike, either staring in amazement at the distasteful sight of beggars or rushing by, pretending not to have noticed the scene. I turned to the woman beside me whose eyes were fixed on the crowds; there was no jealousy in her heart, just a longing to know what life was like on the other side. I extended my vision to her husband; his arms rested on his knees and his head was thrown despairingly into his hands. He reached out to a passer-by, who turned away in disgust, and in anger at rejection, he clenched his fists and threw his body into a lifeless heap.

The cold crept into my bones, my damp jeans clung to my legs and for a time I felt as much an outcast as the couple next to me. I bought them some final nourishment and said goodbye. For some reason from that moment on I rarely had to approach tramps because they would always first approach me. The short-lived moments with such people have taught me many things; to be grateful for all I have, to be content with life and not to be striving constantly for more, and to be aware of the needs of others. At present God does not seem to be opening the door into deeper involvement but I believe there is always purpose and meaning as to why one feels drawn to help particular people.

As I found I was giving more and more of myself, spending many hours every day giving talks, involved in signing sessions or interviews, listening to people's cries, counselling and answering letters, so an emotional and spiritual burnout started to take place. Only the support and encouragement of my church provided me with the inner strength to keep going. After the morning service one Sunday a young lad came to me and asked if we might go somewhere quiet and pray and I thought that perhaps he had a burden on his heart he wanted to share. The burden turned out to be my book! He was conscious of the difficulties I could come up against and wanted to thank God for my willingness to be open and ask that God would use my words mightily. Other people gave me passages from the Bible to read as encouragement.

We ask God to fill you with the knowledge of his will, with all the wisdom and understanding that his Spirit gives. Then you will be able to live as the Lord wants and will always do what pleases Him. Your lives will produce all kinds of good deeds, and you will grow in your knowledge of God. May you be made strong with all the strength which comes from his glorious power, so that you may be able to endure everything with patience. And with joy give thanks to the Father, who has made you fit to have your share of what God has reserved for his people in the kingdom of light (Colossians 1:9-12, GNB).

Then there were the words of gratitude which arrived in letter form from near and far.

I feel privileged to have been given the chance to read your poignant and most compelling book. It is full of sincerity and that is where the keynote lies. It is written from the heart with no pomp and circumstance. Just the simple honest truth. It will be an invaluable and remarkable evidence of life and will I'm sure be of great help to many. I do give you my most sincere congratulations on such a remarkable success. It is indeed rewarding to see such talents and abilities in one so young. But it is no wonder that you were able to utilise your suffering for a more constructive purpose. I do not flatter you, Helena, only tell you the truth from the bottom of my heart. It seems to me that from suffering often strength, courage and wisdom pours to lead us on to a better and richer path of life.

Such words were not only an encouragement but an inspiration to be effective in the work that I was doing. Yet the demands on my life were almost too much and I was not honest enough to share with people around my need for even greater support. As well as feeling the pressure of being put on an emotional and spiritual pedestal, I began to realise that what I was up against was in actual fact a battle. To be working for God and seeing prayers answered and people's lives touched would mean attack from the enemy, and yet it was all so subtle.

Slowly I slid into the depths of depression and negativity. I would walk into the house alone at night, feeling as cold and dark as the weather outside. My eyes filled with tears as emotions of anguish, loneliness, conflict and pain poured out, and I almost felt as if there was something rotting inside me. I had to get rid of it and punish my body. Once more I denied the feeling of hunger, a few pounds down and it felt good. Suddenly a masochistic desire to retreat back into the anorexia arose; the urge to feel again the horror, the degradation and the pain. A voice came thundering into my head, loaded with accusations, and pulling down my self-worth, telling me that I had never been healed of the anorexia in the first place, saying over and over again, 'You can't cope, you're going to mess up all that has been done. You're going to crack.' Feeling torn to shreds and tired, all I could do was cry out to God, 'No! don't let it happen.'

After church one Sunday two of the youth leaders, Steve and Fiona, approached me: 'Is this the big attack we've all been waiting for?' They knew that at some point after the book had been published Satan would take hold of me, like reaching for a damp cloth, and wring every drop of God's promise from my heart; slowly twist me round and round and leave me confused, defaced, scarred and spiritually dry, make me look at the past and believe it to be the present. They had warned me of the inevitability of attack months ago, but I had taken their warning lightly, thinking that I would recognise Satan's stabbing words and cruel accusations; instead I failed to realise who it was and started to walk his path of knives.

Steve and Fiona were not the only ones who had come to the conclusion that in the past week or so I had been under direct Satanic attack. Joan felt the same way. She had been particularly concerned about me as she realised that what I was experiencing was far more than a passing mood; it seemed that I had lost the will to cling onto God's promises or to know His power and strength. She had gone away and prayed and the following night had had a strange dream.

'It was late and dark, about 2.30 a.m. I think. Suddenly the doorbell went and I wondered who on earth could be calling at the Vicarage at that time of night. Slowly I walked towards the door and opened it; you were standing on the doorstep looking worried.'

'"I need to talk Joan," you said.'

'I looked at my watch. "But it's two o'clock in the morning," I replied.'

"I know, but I've just got to talk to you."

'I looked outside to the blackness, the streets were full of prostitutes, and it was evil, horrid out there. I told you I had to find my Bible and you said you wanted to fetch some notes you wanted to show me, so we arranged to meet at a café in town. The café was crowded, dirty, smoky, and full of drunks, tramps and drug addicts. There was nowhere to sit so we stood with our backs pressed against a stone wall. As we talked, I looked at you and you were pale and fragile. Then I noticed a man walking towards us; his face was sinister and terrifying. To my horror I realised he had a flick-knife in his hand and was coming for me. He started attacking me viciously and I looked to you to see if you were going to help me but I realised you couldn't; you were completely powerless. I knocked his hand in defence and the knife fell down the front of my blouse. I was safe; he had lost his weapon. I suggested to you that we left whilst we had the chance, but just as we were going the man came for me again, this time with his nails which were long like daggers. There was no escape so I forced myself to wake up.'

As we sat drinking coffee Joan told me how when she had woken up she had asked God to unravel the meaning of the dream, and He had said to her, 'Helena is in a spiritual battle and you are right in there with her; you have taken care of her, been concerned and prayed, so you too will come under attack.'

Joan turned to me. 'I realised that this had to be prayed over and worked through with you. I was busy Sunday morning, but after lunch I had some time to myself and spent it praying in response to the dream.'

It was amazing because it was that Sunday afternoon, before knowing about the dream, that I had started to feel a sense of freedom. And as Joan and I prayed further I was no longer dragged to the ground by chains which tore painfully into my flesh, but was free. My joy and vitality returned in leaps and bounds and once again I could experience in full God's immeasurable love and the gentleness, beauty and power of the touch of His hand.

The following Sunday the whole of the nine o'clock meeting (an informal church gathering at Greyfriars) was centred on Satanic attack and the need to wait on the Lord. God had laid on someone's heart these words: 'If we are not waiting on the Lord we are vulnerable to attack. He is constantly moving; if we do not keep up, if we stop then we shall trip and fall.'

As an all important question followed, 'Where does your strength lie, with God or with yourself?' I was conscious that I had not taken the battle which Christians are up against seriously.

In the Bible it talks about the devil being like a roaring lion who prowls around seeking someone to devour: well, he had obviously thought I would be very tasty! His teeth had come close to devouring my flesh on this occasion, but never again. I had learnt my lesson, that if

I was to walk in strength it meant putting on the whole armour of God.

Finally, build up your strength in union with the Lord and by the means of his mighty power. Put on all the armour that God gives you, so that you will be able to stand up against the Devil's evil tricks. For we are not fighting against human beings but against the wicked spiritual forces in the heavenly world, the rulers, authorities, and cosmic powers of this dark age. So put on God's armour now! (Ephesians 6:10-13, GNB).

In the days to follow God went on to teach me much about spiritual warfare in a way that would equip and sustain me to continue walking the narrow path. (With hindsight I realise that this was only the beginning of my understanding about warfare and that I would have many more lessons to learn later in life and that the greater my involvement in Christian work the greater the attack would be upon me.)

6

Expression of pain

I saw that helpless look
behind your eyes
that tells of memories
as black as jet
and streaked with blood,
of pain that tore
and tore again your
innocent body apart.

I saw confusion turn
to hate and hate
then flame to guilt;
guilt that burnt
human flesh away
and left a sight
too sore for mortal
eyes to see,
or heart to feel.

It was just as well that I had learnt some lessons about spiritual warfare and the armour of God shortly after *Puppet on a String* was published as I was very quickly thrown into a world of supporting others. Looking back I honestly wonder how I coped in the early stages. Besides working in a hotel I had spent a year working as a crèche assistant, when suddenly one week after *Puppet on a String* was published I was thrown into the role of 'counsellor' and 'mentor', having only completely recovered from the illness myself for fifteen months!

Many of the letters that arrived through the post, or conversations I had with sufferers, started by heartfelt thanks for my having written 'such a compelling and useful book' but were intertwined with desperate pleas for help and requests that someone should understand their pain, difficulties, battle of wills, conundrum of self-identity and fear of getting better.

The more time I spent with people suffering from anorexia, the more insight I gained into this complex illness, and the more I realised, because of the very nature of the emotions involved, how much God was able to help in enabling a victim to recover. It was quite incredible to see how the majority of people mentioned God when they wrote or spoke to me. Some said that since all other help had failed they felt that God was the only answer; others talked about needing God to provide the key to inner happiness. Better still I was to receive a letter from someone who had been completely healed through their faith.

One such letter read,

> I was ill for about six years, from when I was sixteen to when I was twenty-two, at which time I became a Christian. About six months after my commitment I was more severely ill (bulimia) than at any previous point, but at my lowest ebb, the Lord lifted the whole thing from me. I received complete and almost instantaneous healing. That was a year ago, and compared to the rest of my life this last year has been absolutely wonderful. You must know, as I do, the true meaning of being set free. Through the agony of being gripped by such compulsive and alien behaviour, my faith was strengthened, because I knew the true meaning of *slavery* to sin, and I can compare that to the freedom that I now have in Christ!

Over the years of trying to help people suffering from anorexia, I came across people of varying ages and degrees of the problem, from a young child of ten to women in their thirties and from people on the threshold of recovery to those on their death-bed. Each person was so very different, for everyone is an individual, yet there were distinct similarities, not only in background but personality, emotional make-up and ways of coping with life.

In Proverbs 20:5 it says, *'A person's thoughts are like water in a deep well, but someone with insight can draw them out'* (GNB).

I think that the writer of Proverbs says it all. The thoughts of those afflicted by anorexia (and some types of depression or other emotional states) can very much be described as 'like water in a deep well.' Unless someone helps to draw them out they are going to remain like buried poison and the person will go on experiencing confusion and pain.

Confusion and a divided mind (the mind versus the body) are often the first cries that I hear from a person. Obviously it is only those with some desire to pull through who have contacted me, but even so there are mixed feelings of wanting to get better and not wanting to get better. There is still a tug of war between the rational and irrational parts of their mind.

The rational, intellectual mind appreciates that the body has a need and that this need should be fulfilled. This mind can appreciate that my body needs food, that I need to become fatter, that I need a balanced diet. It accepts the limitations of the body and under-stands them. The rational will wants the body to eat. The irrational, emotional will prevents the body from having sufficient nutrients; it makes you starve until you can hardly bear it any longer; it tortures the body – forces it to the limits of endurance at every available opportunity. It degrades the body, scoffs at its limita-tions, pushes it on and on. This is most markedly shown in the eating situation but it applies to other areas of life.[1]

The very nature of anorexia speaks of confusion. The sufferer is exercising incredible self-control in often denying hunger and resisting temptation, showing tremendous inner strength, and yet she holds a childlike frailty and dependence. The two contradict each other.

I often wonder if much of the confusion has to do with the sufferer's apparent inability to identify emotions. A doctor who for several months had been using my book *Puppet on a String* as a means of therapy with his patients once asked me if I felt anorexics were the kind of people

[1] Jill Welbourne and Joan Purgold, *The Eating Sickness. Anorexia, Bulimia and the myth of suicide by slimming*, Harvester Press.

who found it hard to express their emotions. After much discussion we both came to the same conclusion. Yes, anorexics do find it hard to express emotion, especially intense emotion such as love and anger. But there is more to it than that, often they cannot identify a particular emotion. For instance, when asked if they are angry they will say, 'I really don't know'. They may even talk about feeling 'sort of angry'. This creates a state of confusion and indecision. Often when asked to make a decision an anorexic will go into panic and despair. I think a lot of this relates to a crisis about independence and autonomy; an identity crisis.

> We often hear people referring to 'identity crises'. But what does such a term really mean? 'Identity' is best understood as a sense of self which involves both an acknowledgement and acceptance of individuality, of the uniqueness of ourselves, together with the feeling of being part of and accepted by a wider group. An identity crisis occurs when we feel in a great deal of conflict about who we are, both as individual separate people and about where we stand in relation to other people. We all experience this kind of crisis at various points during our lives. It is only when the conflict seems quite impossible for us to resolve that we are likely to deal with it by developing a symptom such as anorexia.[2]

An identity crisis speaks of questioning where a person stands in society, a fear of rejection by others or loss of significance and a lack of self-acceptance. I am sure that at times such conflicts have to do with our upbringing and circumstances during developmental years. Marilyn Lawrence in her book *The Anorexic Experience* talks about how often little girls are brought up to be 'good', that passivity and compliance are qualities which are highly

[2] Marilyn Lawrence, *The Anorexic Experience*, Women's Press.

valued. She goes on to say that whilst compliant, passive daughters may make for a tranquil family life, often it does not lead to a smooth passage to independence.

Parents have often talked about their anorexic daughters as having been 'model children'. Good, compliant and obedient. They have not fought back. Instead they have sat back and accepted things the way they are. Maybe this is half the problem: in being compliant, undemanding (call it what you will), the anorexic has not found her identity or learnt to express feelings; she has failed to develop assertiveness. She wants independence and autonomy, wants to give vent to her aggression, wants to stand up for her rights and yet circumstance or nature have acted as barriers and now these very things frighten her. The result is that the only way to cope with life is for the person to withdraw and retreat into the anorexia shell. Many of the people I have tried to help have expressed the opinion that the anorexic pattern is the only way they know how to cope. One girl in her fight for recovery explains it like this:

When I got back from holiday I was feeling better than I had felt for a long time. Suddenly I found that I was attracting male attention and I found my confidence building up. I wish I could be self-confident as those few tastes of it made me want to be permanently that way. But I'm not, and at the moment my decision stands to withdraw again. It's the safest way I know, as sometimes I feel too fragile for the hurts that come with coping with life. When I was ill I was so numb that I hardly felt pain. I just feel so insecure now. When I was emaciated it seemed to cut me off from life and I just existed in a half-life. That may sound pretty bad but actually it helped me hide away. I just can't seem to stop wanting to crawl back into that hole again. I guess I'm just a very confused person at the moment. It's the only way I know how to cope with life.

Through anorexia the person is in some ways putting up a façade of self-sufficiency: 'I don't need other people; I can crawl into my anorexic hole and let the world mind its own business,' while underneath, if first they can drop the guard of self-sufficiency and show true feeling, a great deal of insecurity sits slowly turning bad. The depth of insecurity experienced was once expressed to me by the same girl who had so beautifully described the numbness of anorexia as the only way she knew how to cope with the hurts of life.

> When I was admitted to hospital I was very close to death. I could feel it. It was like going back to childhood, even babyhood to try and capture a sense of security. At my worst time I felt so helpless and lay on my bed in a foetal position. As I slowly got better I liked to wear socks in bed because it made me feel more secure – like a baby.

Feelings of insecurity seem to be very strong in anorexia. Maybe that is why it is those who have come to know the Lord who have recovered, because they have found their security in Him.

Insecurity seems to stimulate a lack of self-confidence and low self-worth. 'Anorexia is a symptom which can only flourish in the woman who lacks self-confidence and who has not found a way of being in the world which is both comfortable and realistic. She is a woman who cannot ask for the help and support she needs, but who experiences herself as incompetent if she cannot, alone, achieve perfection. The recovered anorexic, on the other hand is able to feel at home in the world, to evaluate herself realistically and let go of her need to be lonely and perfect.'[3]

Anorexics are some of the most perfectionist people I

[3] Marilyn Lawrence, *The Anorexic Experience*, Women's Press.

have seen and I wonder if rather than perfectionism being a symptom of anorexia, it is a cause. Anorexia seems to have a lot to do with expectation, the setting of unrealistic standards and high achievement. When I look back I can see that during my teens my mind was centred on achievement, standards and lack of failure to such an extent that the 'normal' way of behaviour during adolescence was virtually non-existent. I was not 'silly' or 'giggly' or interested in dating, discos or makeup. Instead there was an unhealthy seriousness about life. Older people, looking at me, would often relate to my 'deep thinking' as 'a maturity beyond my years'. But as I look back on my experience with hindsight and the more I come to know of other anorexics' behaviour, the greater the realisation that it is these perfectionist, striving and serious teenagers that are at great risk of developing illnesses such as anorexia.

The anorexic lives under a thick cloud of fear of failure. She wants to achieve perfection, wants to prove her perfectionism to others and lives in fear of it being discovered that she is not perfect. The desire for a low body weight is tied in with the desire for perfection, but sadly the lower she gets the greater the realisation that her task has not been accomplished. In reality perfectionism equates zero on the scales, because zero means that she will have done away with failure. Some people have talked about anorexia as a 'slow form of suicide'. I believe there is truth in this inasmuch as suicide is an attempt at doing away with a part of life that is not acceptable to the person. Amongst other things the anorexic is trying to do away with imperfection and failure.

The authors of the book *The Eating Sickness*,[4] make what I consider to be a very valid point in effectively

---

[4] Jill Welbourne and Joan Purgold, *The Eating Sickness. Anorexia, Bulimia and the myth of suicide by slimming*, Harvester Press

saying that the anorexic reduces her body size to fit her diminished sense of self.

Selwyn Hughes in his study notes, *Every Day with Jesus*, describes perfectionism as a constant feeling of never doing well enough. He says, 'The feeling permeates all of life, but especially affects our spiritual life. It is akin to inferiority, but really quite different from it. While on the surface they may look alike, there is a gulf between them. Inferiority says "I *can't* do better" – perfectionism says, "I *ought* to do better." Psychologist Karen Horney's classic phrase describes it perfectly: "The tyranny of the *oughts*".'

One of the girls I have been involved with in counselling through correspondence over a couple of years is a prime example of someone locked into perfectionism. I have used extracts from Elizabeth's initial letter to me on various occasions as an example of how unresolved emotional conflict can hold a person in captivity.

Dear Helena

I have read your excellent book *Puppet on a String* twice and found it quite relieving to read about another anorexic's problems and relating them to my own. I am, at the moment, being treated for anorexia nervosa at the age of fourteen. Last year I was in hospital twice, the first time for five weeks, the second time for nine weeks.

I suffered the same negative thoughts and depression as you, though perhaps not so badly.

I feel fat a lot of the time and think that I am ugly. I find it hard to believe that anyone can love me. I think myself cruel and selfish towards my parents and blame myself for almost every argument or bad incident.

I cannot talk about the illness with my friends, as I think that they will assume I am overacting or stupid and stubborn. Therefore I spend much time wrapped up with the problem, unable to counteract it.

Although I go to church and believe in God and Jesus, I find it difficult to pray or ask for guidance and help. He is not there, or so it seems anyway. Especially since my grandmother and a very special friend, John, died relatively close to each other. John's death especially hurt, as he was only thirteen and had helped me in hospital. After his death I wanted to give up and die also to be with my friend. I only kept going because of his memory. Now, when I think of him or remember the good times we had in hospital I cry a lot. It seems too much. I blame myself for his death because when I returned to school I felt dejected and left out. I wished something would happen that would make people feel sorry for me. My grandmother was also ill at the time and I thought horrid things like, 'If Gran or John died, perhaps people would comfort me.' Both of them died shortly afterwards and I felt so nasty, like a murderer.

I am writing to you because I want to tell my feelings and innermost thoughts to someone who has suffered very similar occurrences.

Thank you for your book, it helped me.

Her second letter, which quickly followed my reply, gave even more indication as to what lay behind the anorexia.

The doctors and I have spent quite a long time trying to uncover the reason for my illness. We have come to the conclusion that there were many small causes. I have a very intelligent brother. He has always done outstandingly well at school, and whilst being pleased, occasionally I have felt a great inadequacy at not doing so well. Many times I felt unloved and always walking in his shadow; my achievements being obliterated by everything he has done. In addition to this sometimes I felt rejected and left out by friends.

My fear of fat is preventing my recovery and also a feeling that people will again reject me and not notice me. Common sense ought to tell me that I am under-weight, but it doesn't. I feel fat and bloated.

A few months later Elizabeth again expressed her feeling of failure and inability to accept any change in her weight.

My weight is still a terrible problem to me. I just cannot accept any increase no matter how hard I try. Often I get bouts of tearful depression, it is a horrible feeling.

I have a terrible fear of being left out; it sends me into a cruel fog on occasions. I am very sensitive and hate people being overtly hurtful to me. I often experi-ence a sense of failure. At times I detest myself for the way I treat my mother; I claw at my face and scream inwardly.

I feel quite strongly that it is in God that self-acceptance can be found, the fear of failure overcome, and the need for perfection diminished. With each letter that came Elizabeth's realisation of this seemed to grow but her fear of getting better was so strong it seemed almost too difficult to let God in. She could see that Christians around her had something that she lacked and in one letter said, 'Please help me to find God. I know that is a terrible thing to say because it is only me who can change my attitude, but I try to understand what He wants me to do.'

Nearly two years after her first letter, Elizabeth used the word 'perfectionist' for the first time. She said that although she realised she had a long way to go before recovery she considered herself over the worst of it. Even so, she said, 'I have to admit that I am still a perfectionist. It is really terrible, I feel I have to succeed at everything. I am so upset if I do not do well in a subject at school.'

Her perfectionist way of thinking was preventing a breakthrough.

Perfectionism is extremely troublesome because it is inextricably connected to several other problems. It is linked, for example, to low self-esteem. If you are never quite satisfied with yourself and your achievements, then your conclusion is that God isn't satisfied with you either. So back you go into the spiritual salt-mines to try to work yourself into His good books.

Perfectionism is linked also to legalism. The over-sensitive conscience of the perfectionist is usually accompanied by great scrupulosity which rigidly over-emphasises external do's and don'ts, rules and regulations. Perfectionism is connected too, with guilt. The perfectionist thinks that God is against him for his sin, rather than for him against his sin.

Finally, perfectionism is linked to anger. Most perfectionists are angry people – not on the surface, but deep down inside. They unconsciously resent the 'oughts' of life, and develop a dislike of God. This anger is often repressed and denied, with the result that deep emotional problems begin to set in.[5]

The anorexic's perfectionism leads to a rigid self-control: they consider loss of control as failure. The very thought creates a deep-set fear, fear that the minute the slightest self-control is lost all control will disappear and they will be forced to the depths of self-indulgence. Guilt acts as a deadly reminder that indulgence of even the smallest amount is the ultimate sin and 'giving in' is a sign of complete and utter uselessness.

[5] Selwyn Hughes, *Every Day with Jesus*, CWR, May/June 1984

When trying to help people overcome perfectionism and let go of their iron control it is extremely difficult to put into words practical steps, maybe because it has a lot to do with self-realisation: a process that no one other than the person is able to work through. Other people can be a support, encouragement, director of steps and shoulder on which to cry, but when it comes to the crunch only the one afflicted can make the decision to work at it.

For me, release came when I found my security in God, recognising His unconditional love and realising that I did not need to be perfect. I began to see that perfectionism was in fact a hindrance. Even so, perfectionism was a part of my personality and it took a lot of determination to 'let go'. Some people would say that I am still a perfectionist; in many ways I am: I like to do a job well, but the difference is that I am no longer in bondage to it. In order for that to happen I had to 'allow myself' to mess things up, and then see that, in fact, it did not really matter. I could laugh, along with other people about the stupidity of my mistake, and what a wonderful feeling and release of tension! As I began to 'let go' of the perfectionism I discovered that life was about laughter as well as tears; I lost that unhealthy seriousness about life. I could even accept a compliment without thinking, 'there has to be some trick behind this!'

My only answer to the problem of perfectionism is to trust God and make a concerted effort to know Him in a deeper way. That means spending time reading the Bible, because it is there that truths about Him are found. Many perfectionists have difficulty in accepting God because they have the misconceived idea that God's love is conditional on their achievements and that He is always expecting more of them. Not so, perfectionists expect more of themselves. God loves despite everything. He does not love us for what we accomplish but for who we are.

Just as overcoming perfectionism is a fight, so too recovery from the whole of anorexia is rather like walking into the battlefield with only one's own determination as a means of self-defence. One of the people I was in correspondence with for some time, in struggling to recover, said:

Help! People are starting to tell me how much better I am looking and it sends me to look so critically at myself in the mirror and I get so despondent I want to take five steps backward for that one forward, but I turn to your book and re-read the part where two friends at your course tell you you looked better having gained a bit of weight, and I think of your reaction. It is all so true to form. Did/do you eventually come to terms with it? Sometimes I see a spark of light by saying to myself, what is more important, to have a life of my own or just an existence, it takes a lot of building back doesn't it?

My purpose in replying to her letter was to try to keep up her determination to win. Anorexics are very strong people. They have to be to go through all they do. If only their strength can be channelled into recovery, not the temptation to revert back into the old patterns, they have a chance.

I know that terrible feeling when people start to tell you how much better you look and suddenly all your defence mechanisms start to jump into action,' I replied. 'To begin with "better" represents something bad, it means you've failed, you've lost control, you are heading towards that even more dreaded word, "normality". You are bound to feel like taking five steps backwards. If you didn't, things would be too easy, there would be no battle and you would be over the whole thing tomorrow. The important thing at this stage is not to panic; not to feel threatened by that word, "better". It doesn't represent fat, unable to cope, lack of self-control and lack of self-confidence. It represents beauty, personality change, emotional stability, self-control, self-confidence, joy, and much, much more. Sure enough it's hard work but soon your reaction will change. Whatever happens, don't give up hoping or give up battling.

I went on to talk about the difficulties over mealtimes, the importance of focusing on things other than food, to become more outward-looking and about ways in which to try to mix with people and thus develop self-confidence. The reply that followed a few weeks later gave incredible insight into the struggle that those caught in emotional conflict have in facing a normal life again. But how worthwhile it is to win!

It is too easy for people caught in the trap of problems such as anorexia to be content with half-recovery. Part of one of my letters in reply to such a situation read:

Sometimes I think anorexia is very similar to the different seasons. At your worst you are deep in snow; cold, miserable, want to shut yourself inside, even wish you could go to sleep until spring or summer arrives. At times you even enjoy that sensation of being snug inside and using the weather as an excuse for not venturing out. Then comes that first glimmer of hope, a clear blue sky, a few golden rays of sunshine and at long last the spring flowers begin to push their way through the hardened earth – symbols of life and examples of beauty. For once you have the desire to take a walk; as you look around so there is more evidence of spring; delicate pink blossom, brilliant new green leaves, birds singing melodiously. Suddenly you realise how much you appreciate the evidence of new life and how you would hate to be back in the middle of winter again. But still there are cold days, days when your hope is suddenly dashed – even so something keeps you plodding on. Without realising summer gradually creeps up on you; lighter evenings, sun and warmth; activity, enthusiasm and joy all naturally flow. When you feel the heat pour over your body like liquid gold, you find it hard to imagine what it was like to be deep in snow and ice and feeling bitterly cold.

Anorexia is a process, and like many other processes there is a lot of effort needed in order to reach the next stage. What I would like to ask you is, are you moving forward? Or are you content to stay where you are – well enough to have a job and socialise a little but still remaining at a 'safe' (low) weight, and not really experiencing life at its best? Which would you prefer – spring with its darker nights and at times pretty cold days or summer with lighter evenings, sun and warmth?

It's too easy to stay in that in-between stage, 'better' but not 'cured'. Now is your chance to change that. I know it is hard and seemingly painfully slow, but believe me it's worthwhile, and in time you will realise that this whole experience has made you a stronger person. Now is the time to decide whether anorexia is going to make or break you. Your mother is right when she talks about positive thinking. It is so important. Positive thinking is all about getting life into perspective and life into perspective is all about putting God first, and putting God first is all about trust and obedience, and trust and obedience result in peace, joy and self-acceptance.

Psalm 62:5-8, sums it all up:

> *I depend on God alone;*
> *I put my hope in him.*
> *He alone protects and saves me;*

> *he is my defender,*
> *and I shall never be defeated.*
> *My salvation and honour depend on God;*
> *he is my strong protector;*
> *he is my shelter.*
> *Trust in God at all times my people.*
> *Tell him all your troubles,*
> *for he is our refuge.*

(GNB)

In so many cases it appears to be those people who have come to know God who have found release, but it is not uncommon, in the early stages, for a person to belittle their faith just as they put themselves down. My answer to that is, 'You say that you still question whether your faith is strong enough. It is. In Luke 17:6 it says, *If you had faith as big as a mustard seed, you could say to this mulberry tree, 'Pull yourself up by the roots and plant yourself in the sea!' and it would obey you.'* (GNB). It is not that we have loved God but that He loved us, and therefore He delights to give us the gift of faith. We can't create or earn faith, all we can be are channels for Him to work through. So, yes, your faith is strong enough, and you must believe this because it is as we put our faith into practice that we start to see amazing things happening.'

In the few years of helping anorexics I have indeed seen amazing things happen. One girl came to me depressed and locked into anorexia: she was a severe case, had received endless treatment by psychiatrists over several years, had attempted suicide on more than one occasion and was very self-destructive. We talked, and whilst it appeared to relieve some tension, nothing changed. It was not until quite some months later that she said, 'I feel that I have got the devil right inside of me.' With that she asked if I would pray for her. I prayed very simply but I felt God's presence in the room in a way that I had never experienced before. There also seemed to be a sparkle in her eyes that had previously not been there. Nearly six months later I received a phone call which told me that she was up at a normal weight but panicking. I gave her some practical advice and asked friends to pray. Only a week after that I received another phone call to say that all fear and guilt had gone. She felt completely better and wanted to help others going through the turmoil that had once been hers. She sounded a completely different person and the last time I saw her she looked a completely different person!

I could write of many other similar stories, but this is not a book on anorexia but rather a book of how God opens doors and changes lives. The significant fact is that people do recover and if God can touch the heart of someone suffering from anorexia and make a drastic change in her life, He can also touch the hearts of people caught in other negative emotional states and heal them.

7

Feelings

Empty, lonely
distant and far,
who knows the pain
of an unhealed scar?
Who's seen the effects
of memories return
where flames of anguish
can burn and burn?
Who knows the feeling
of hope torn away
yet hides the hurt
by what they say?
And who has felt
so desperate inside
to live means
simply to hide.

Being thrown into a world of helping others as a result of writing about my own experience of anorexia, I realised that it was important to continue to address my own issues. (Though little did I realise that years later this would mean major emotional surgery, but that is another book!). After coming through anorexia, whilst I was aware that life would not necessarily be easy, I was nevertheless surprised at the onslaught of suffering that came my way. As well as Kathie's death and my broken engagement, I carried around with me a thorn in the flesh – a problem that I had had since birth and which I had never managed to come to terms with. In addition to that there remained a few painful situations that I had not been able to hand over to God and an ongoing battle with depression.

The thorn in my flesh was an eye defect that I had had since birth. I had been born blind and at only a few months old my mother realised that there was something wrong and later investigations by an eye specialist proved that I had a severe nystagmus. The condition improved until I was about nine and then stabilised, still leaving me with great difficulty in focusing and seeing anything that was not close at hand. I had grown up that way and so knowing no different had learnt to adapt and cope, just like some people walk around with a limp. Outwardly it did not appear to affect my life. I could still take part in childish feats, come top in high jump and long jump and even be goal-shooter in the netball team. However it did cause problems, especially when I was too bashful to tell teachers that I could not read what was written on the blackboard despite being at the front of the class. Being incredibly shy and hating people asking me what the problem with my eyes was, I would rather be reprimanded for doing badly in class than stand out as different. Then there were countless occasions when I finally plucked up the courage to tell a teacher only to be told that I was making excuses and the horrendous bullying that accompanied being vulnerable. Medically I did not understand exactly what was wrong with my eyes and so tended to avoid the issue when asked. The result was that over the years I built up a defence mechanism which enabled me never to talk about it.

The topic did not really come out into the open again until my late teens when friends all around me were learning to drive and being given freedom and independence, and I was having to accept that I would never have that freedom. Feelings had been suppressed for so long and locked deep inside that when I was faced with hard truths such as not being able to drive I knew logically that there was frustration, anger and bitterness bubbling away within me, but felt nothing other than a sense of powerlessness. I found it difficult to handle when I saw friends, younger than myself, driving home after church whilst I was left hunting for a lift or amidst deep conversation I would be conscious of someone shouting, 'Your mother's waiting outside'. Sometimes I would choose to cycle or walk through Reading late at night in order to have some social life, only to be told by people how dangerous the streets were and how stupid I was. I wanted to shout back at them and say, 'Do you want me to sit and stifle in my own company or keep my sanity?' Instead I would swallow my words and bury the feelings.

I do not think people realised the pain involved; how much it hurt to see other people's independence and the inconvenience caused by often not being able to read departure times or alterations at railway stations and airports. A part of that pain was justified and very real, but an even bigger part was envy and jealousy and I knew it was wrong. I knew how much bitterness I could harbour, and how I could so easily let self-pity step in and take over. It made me feel so bad and I was becoming ever more conscious that I needed to ask God's help in changing my attitude and healing the pain. Before I could do that though, it was necessary for me to have an openness and honesty with other people.

The most obvious person with whom to talk it through was Joan, who had been a tower of strength ever since I had joined the young people's group at Greyfriars Church. We mulled over the problem and she suggested I phone up Peter, an eye specialist who was a member of the church.

Several months passed before Joan helped me to make an appointment with Peter in his clinic. Within that time I had had my annual appointment at the eye clinic at the Royal Berkshire Hospital. I lived in fear of it every year and regarded the hours of waiting around in the out-patients as a waste of time. But on this occasion I was hoping that the hours I had spent praying for healing were going to show a definite improvement and leave the doctor standing back in amazement! Not so. After the tests were over I asked the doctor if there was any change. The answer was 'no' – in fact, I was slightly more short-sighted in the left eye than last time. Disappointment flooded my body. It seemed so unfair, so cruel. I tried to push aside the bad feelings, which were becoming stronger by the minute, but it was to no avail. I asked a few questions and left the room.

The following Sunday I wanted to share with the people at church the disappointment I had experienced, but I found that I was powerless to open my mouth. But

God's call was so strong I could not ignore it, and stumbling over my words, I spoke. During the meeting I was conscious of God telling me something of great importance: for healing to take place (physical or emotional) it was necessary for me to forgive all those in the past connected with my eyesight. Not until that day did I realise the extent of the bitterness I was harbouring. Only a few weeks previously I had been at a Christian convention, where I was asked to participate in the authors' and artists' evening, and heard Selwyn Hughes speak on healing life's hurts. He talked about us desperately wanting to receive healing from God, and God's desire to give us that healing. 'But,' he said, 'it is as though in the palms of our hands there is a scar, and as we reach out and clasp the healing that scar re-opens and causes much pain – we quickly take our hand back because it is too painful to hold on any longer.' This made me realise the preparation needed for healing. Already I was conscious of an emotional healing taking place. If God wanted to heal me physically as well that was up to Him!

With emotional healing having started I was in a far more rational and less sensitive state by the time my appointment with Peter arrived. Joan had said that she would come with me and I insisted she came right into the room, no staying outside! I explained my history to Peter and told him that my greatest sadness was that I could not drive. He looked at me and said, 'Okay, let's see what we can do. What can you read on that board?'

I gave it a quick glance and replied, 'Not a lot!'

He seemed surprised and must have thought that I was having him on. 'It can't be that bad, start at the top.'

I started at the top, the trouble was I did not get much further! With my right eye I could only read the first letter, and with my left eye I couldn't even see that there was a chart on the wall! He tried various combinations of lenses, there was a slight improvement, but nothing to write home about. I looked and looked, I opened my eyes wide, I shut them, I leaned forward, still the world did not change. He tried half a dozen more combinations, after each one I said, 'No different.'

I smiled a little to make it look as if it was a bit of a joke. But inside I hurt deeply.

He looked at me sadly, 'I'm sorry Helena. I don't think you are going to be able to drive. You need to be capable of reading to that red line.' The line was a red blur to me and I could tell that there were dozens more letters between my efforts and that hateful line! I forced back all evidence of tears.

'You have done marvellously to get where you have,' Peter said, 'In fact you have done well to get through school and college; you must be a very determined person.'

I smiled. Joan stepped in, 'She *is* very determined.'

I suppose that's it, I thought, and was just about to stand up when Peter spoke again. 'Remember, for Christians it is different. We may not understand why God allows us to go through these things, but we have to trust Him. He has a reason, a purpose for our good, and He is not beyond performing a miracle of healing. All I can say, Helena, is that I am very sorry, and any improvement will be nothing short of a miracle.'

I wait for that miracle and in the meantime, keep surrendering to God the pain and inconvenience of being partially sighted.

Not only did God take me to the place of beginning to deal with the reality of my eyesight, but for months after I had become a Christian and recovered from anorexia, He showed me things in my life which needed to be dealt with – attitudes and at times memories. Much of my childhood had remained locked up (its uncovering may one day be another book) but occasionally there would be memories. One such memory was an event that happened when I was seventeen whilst doing a summer job. It was six weeks of on-going sexual harassment, abuse and attempted rape. At that time I was already very fearful of men but didn't know why.

As the memories re-emerged I knew that I had to deal with them. Suppressing them only resulted in my drawing further and further away from God. I built barriers in my relationship with God and with other people and then tried to fill the empty hole that had been created with things of the world, but these did not produce the same satisfaction as being close to the Lord or close to Christian friends.

Arriving at the nine o'clock meeting at Greyfriars one Sunday, I told God how I was becoming conscious of some past events. I prayed that He would do something to change my negativity and desire to hide away. The theme of the meeting was healing and one of the leaders asked if anyone present needed prayer for anything specific. No one spoke.

'Okay,' he said, 'if no one else wants prayer for healing, you can pray for me. I have had rumblings of another kidney stone, and I don't want to go through that same terrible pain.'

He stopped speaking and people started praying. When he had had the same problem about a year previously God had healed him, so people were expectant. After they had finished praying he went on to give an analogy, 'Some here are cold and hard like stones'.

I looked at my feet in shame. I knew that was a pretty good description of me at that moment.

'A kidney stone is only small but it can cause incredible pain. If you harbour any pain it is important that you deal with it *now*, otherwise it will only get worse.'

I realised that there was truth in what he was saying, but I felt unable to cope with anything other than that which was superficial, and so began to feel very uncomfortable. I buried my head in my hands and decided that

I must leave the room as soon as possible. Just as I was about to get up and leave someone had a word of prophecy for me ...

Helena, I want you to receive my healing. I want you to take hold of it but you hide away. You hold on to the tree of bitterness and the tree of resentment. You have hurts and fears that you bury. Give them to me; let me take from you your pain, your bitterness and resentment and give you my love and joy.'

As the words were spoken I wept. The person who had spoken them knew nothing of my feelings, in fact no one knew of the oppression, pain and resentment. Only God knew, and being aware of the extent of it he could not bear to let me sit back and suffer. Someone else went on to speak further words of prophecy:

I want to fill you with my peace and joy. I want to give you my love, so that you can give it to others. Lift up your head, my child, wipe away your tears, look at me, look at my face.

I found it hard to let go of the hurt and resentment that had built up inside me, but God finally got through to me when I joined the other leaders and assistant leaders of Crossroads at a weekend conference. The conference was entitled 'Battle Stations'.

The first seminar I attended had the wonderful title, 'The problem of crisis without process'. The speaker started by saying that most of the experiences we go through are make or break experiences. When we go through a crisis we have to choose between walking along the three-lane highway or the narrow road. Many people go through the crisis but they do not carry on with the process; they make the decision but they do not continue. He said that crisis without process is terrible; it is like going through a black tunnel and never coming out the other side.

I began to feel greatly challenged. I had my 'crisis', in recounting the happenings of the summer job; the question remained, was I going to go through with the 'process', the healing? Only I could decide.

In the afternoon meeting, entitled 'Living in revival', I was challenged still further. The speaker pointed to two doors behind him, one said 'private' the other said 'push'. 'Which sign is it you are going to put up on your door?' he asked.

As he talked, the cogs in my mind whizzed round. Every now and again a sentence would shout out at me; the words repeating themselves over and over again.

'Revival has to start with where we are with the Lord.'

Right now, not very close, I thought.

'We need more of God in our lives and less of self.' The speaker continued. 'We need a new cleansing and a new heart. A heart of stone replaced by a heart of flesh. God is not concerned with empty words and empty actions. We need Him to melt our hearts.'

Finally, he said that once God has melted our hearts He will give us a new spirit.

All that the speaker was saying was echoing the words spoken at the nine o'clock meeting the Sunday that God touched me so deeply.

In the evening meeting God was working in power, in a way I had never witnessed before. Several of the speakers were moving amongst people and praying for them. One of them came over to me, placed both hands on my shoulders and then proceeded to have a word of knowledge about me feeling unworthy of God's love and how God wanted to heal the pain and bitterness that was within. Tears flowed as this complete stranger spoke of how I felt and what God was doing. I wept bitterly: it hurt so much. Then in the next half-hour God took me visually through each scene that had caused me heartache and showed me where He was at that time, revealing the depth of His love. At the end all guilt and pain were washed away and I felt exhausted but wonderfully blessed.

The nine o'clock meeting the following week was a continuation and confirmation of healing and infilling, and I was able to share with the others a little of how God had touched me. Every verse I read in the Bible seemed to hold new meaning; every prayer prayed was like an intense thirst being quenched.

8

Broken and bleeding

I lie broken and bleeding,
torn to shreds,
crying in agony.
My body thrashes around,
heaves and pulsates,
is thrown on to dry
and desolate land
and left to shrivel up.
Tears flow down my cheeks
in an endless stream,
on and on until there is
no moisture left inside.
Will I ever understand?

There was a time in my life, when I felt that I had suffered quite enough, and was determined from that moment to show to others *only* my strengths, *not* my weaknesses: to paint all over myself a veneer of joy and to wear a mask depicting a continual smile. I thought that was what other people wanted to see; that they would respect someone who was always strong and happy. The trouble was that less than two months after my decision to live like this I entered the most intense inner pain and depression I have ever experienced. My veneer was stripped off, and my mask fell crashing to the ground and lay in dozens of useless pieces.

I often wonder if God allowed me to go through this experience to show that it is more important to be real than strong. One thing is for sure, those few months of pain have proved to be some of the most vital months of my life; with so many lessons and truths learned that I feel I grew ten-fold in my understanding of living.

The depression was not something that suddenly leapt upon me in the dark, but something I slid into slowly and subtly. I had experienced periods of depression since I was thirteen and had tasted enough of it to know that it was not something I wanted to experience often! At first when the depression took hold of me I could hardly put into words how I felt. The only words that held any meaning were 'pain' and 'screaming in agony'. It was as much as I could do to get through work, and then coming home in the afternoon I would open the front door, feel a wave of inexplicable emptiness and loss, and break down.

My only solace was in reading the Psalms and realising that David knew how I felt and could express it in words that I was at a loss to find.

I am bent and bowed down greatly; I go about mourning all the day long. For my loins are filled with burning, and there is no soundness in my flesh. I am faint and sorely bruised – deadly cold and quite worn out; I groan by reason of the disquiet and moaning of my heart. Lord, all my desire is before You, and my sighing is not hid from You. My heart throbs, my strength fails me.

For I am ready to halt and fall; my pain and sorrow are continually before me.

Forsake me not, O Lord; O my God, be not far from me. Make haste to help me, O Lord, my salvation. (Psalm 38:6-10a, 17, 21-22, The Amplified Bible).

It was always a comfort to read verses from the Bible; on many occasions I felt that particular words had been written just for me. But at my worst the motivation to pick up the Bible and flick through the passages I had underlined in red was not there, and if I did actually manage to open up a page my eyes would be too tear-filled to make sense of the words.

At such times what I feared most was aloneness and yet I would find myself intensifying the pain by isolating myself from God and other people. I was torn to shreds and longed to be with someone and know their care, yet I could not bring myself to ask. The fear of being a burden and showing my weakness was too great. I rode around on my bike in the dark at high speed; hoping that the cold and wind would blow away the negativity and give me new life. It did not happen and I sat outside a friend's house, staring, waiting, wondering; not daring to ring the bell. I realised that there was nothing anybody could do, this was something I was going to have to work through on my own. So, solemnly I returned home. As soon as I opened the door tears flooded once again and I was brought to that desperate point of vulnerability.

On occasions I may have isolated myself from God and others and experienced utter aloneness, but it did not stop God from speaking to me. In the first few weeks of the depression, He spoke some very meaningful words:

There is much you do not understand, there is much pain and searching that you are going through. Take my hand and walk through these with *me*. For they are lessons I need to teach you. But not lessons where you will walk alone. I have chosen you and I choose to work on you in new ways; ways that at times may be costly, but have you not trusted me in the past and seen my creation? So trust me now. I will not test you beyond your limits. Hold on to the promises I have given you; promises that reveal my love for you.

What I have given you I will not take away. I have filled you with my Spirit and bestowed upon you gifts to be used in honour of My name. Do not waste all that I have done for you.

Remember this, gold is precious, but it is necessary for it to pass through the refiner's fire. When it passes through it is not destroyed; it is not even damaged or scarred. You are like gold to me. Listen to My words – the flames will not destroy; they will test and they will cleanse. There is indeed pain, but a pain that is not wasted; a pain that one day will bear fruit.

Several weeks of anguish passed before I realised that I was never going to be able to fight the pain alone. One Sunday, after the evening service, I was returning a book to Joan, when she sensed something was wrong and said that we must pray together. With all the usual activities going on around, the only possible place to pray was a darkened church after everyone else had left. Joan and another friend, Ro, sat either side of me and prayed. Then they urged me to pray. I couldn't; the pain had overwhelmed me and I could do nothing. Many questions were asked. I remember little, except that Joan and Ro were encouraging me to express emotion. Joan said she felt that I needed to show anger and yet, she said, it seemed that I did not even know what anger was or how to express it. She had touched on a vital point. Over the weeks to come more and more things pointed to how for years I had numbed my real feelings and was taken over by depression. They urged me to be open about how I felt and talked of how all of us have child and adult in us and when threatened or hurt we have a choice either to act the way of the child, which is to be irrational and emotional, or to act the way of the adult, standing back and being objective.

So much of what they said made sense and yet I felt powerless to do anything because the pain was almost like a force that swept through my body. When they left I found myself in even deeper depression because suddenly I had been flung into that dreaded situation of aloneness and abandonment.

There were two important factors behind the depression at that time: separation anxiety, from babyhood, and a complete inability to identify feelings. In addition I was able to pinpoint factors in my life that were a stress, such as a fear of loss of identity and integrity or becoming meaningless to people; a fear of aloneness, and the inability to handle being misunderstood.

Although there were far greater complexities behind my depression than I could deal with at the time, God had none the less started a healing work, which continued when I went to Spring Harvest. At the opening celebration the speaker told us to spend a short time in silent prayer bringing before God any burdens or situations that we had carried with us. In the quietness of my heart I laid the burden of my depression before God.

One of the first seminars was on compassion: the words challenged me deeply, 'Love cannot be a silent or stagnant thing; it motivates us into action.' There followed a description of agape love; complete, self-giving love. I knew that it was going to be this sacrificial love that soon would wipe away my pain and restore my enthusiasm and vitality.

Throughout the day, and through words spoken, my conscience told me that I needed to become grounded in my faith. It spoke to me of the necessity for greater depth in my relationship with God and people close to me.

In the hours which followed God spoke to me with power when on opening my Bible I stumbled across Isaiah 60:1. *'ARISE (from the depression and prostration in which circumstances have kept you; rise to a new life)! Shine – be radiant with the glory of the Lord for your light is come, and the glory of the Lord is risen upon you!'* (The Amplified Bible).

Part of the trouble had been that whilst in the pain I found it impossible to pray, worship God or even feel His love. In a worship seminar led by Graham Kendrick, those barriers started to break down. Graham talked about motivation and the fact that when our circumstances / mood do not call us to worship we need to discipline ourselves, have determination to delight in the Lord for who He is. 'The will alone cannot produce worship. Only the Holy Spirit can ignite the flame. We come as the candle, which the Holy Spirit sets alight.' He went on to say something that has proved to be one of my greatest discoveries: 'Worship is far more than joy – we need to bring before God our tears and grief.' It was an absolute revelation to me that besides praise, brokenness is valid in worship.

As Graham pointed out, probably one of Jesus' most

powerful times of worship was in the garden of Gethsemane when he had cried out in great depth to the Father to take the cup of suffering from Him, but ended by saying, in total submission, 'Yet not my will but yours be done.' At that point he was in complete communion with the Father, and in brokenness entered a tremendous time of worship.

Gradually I began to experience that freedom of worship. I was still caught in the same severe pain but as we sang songs of being wholly available, a true giving of ourselves, I wept and worshipped. The main difference was that I was beginning to bring God into my pain instead of declaring it too ugly for Him or anyone else to look at.

After weeping until the early hours I prayed that God would minister to me in my sleep. I woke feeling refreshed and alert to listen to Ian Barclay give an excellent Bible study on John 15. 'Pruning is the way of producing luscious fruit. Pain, sorrow, suffering and grief are part of that process.' He gave an example from C.S. Lewis' book, *The Voyage of the Dawn Treader*, of the way in which pain can be used to prune.

Eustace, one of the boys, has turned into a dragon. He tries and tries to remove the dragon-skin himself; each attempt, though painless, fails. Then he hears Aslan, the lion (who represents Jesus), speak. Later, he tells Edmund:

'Then the lion said – but I don't know if it spoke – "You will have to let me undress you." I was afraid of his claws, I can tell you, but I was pretty nearly desperate now. So I just lay flat down on my back to let him do it.

'The very first tear he made was so deep that I thought it had gone right into my heart. And when he began pulling the skin off, it hurt worse than anything I've ever felt. The only thing that made me able to bear it was just the pleasure of feeling the stuff peel off. You know – if you've ever picked a scab off a sore place. It hurts like billy – oh but it *is* such fun to see it coming away.

'I know exactly what you mean,' said Edmund.

'Well, he peeled the beastly stuff right off – just as I thought it myself the other three times, only they hadn't hurt – and there it was lying on the grass: only ever so much thicker, and darker, and more knobbly-looking than the others had been. And there was I as smooth and soft as a peeled switch and smaller than I had been. Then he caught hold of me – I didn't like that much for I was very tender underneath now that I'd no skin on – and threw me in to the water. It smarted like anything but only for a moment. After that it became perfectly delicious and as soon as I started swimming and splashing I found that all the pain had gone from my arm. And then I saw why. I'd turned into a boy again.'[6]

I could not believe how almost every seminar I attended spoke deeply to me about the pain I was in. After listening to what Ian Barclay had to say about pruning, I attended a special seminar on suffering. The speaker quoted from Deuteronomy 8, which talked of being led into the wilderness to be humbled and to prove exactly what is in our hearts and minds.

Sometimes *all* we have to offer God is a broken and contrite heart. But in that *offering* God transforms our suffering into good. One thing I began to learn was the part that sacrifice (offering) has to play. In the Old Testament sacrifice often took place, whereas in modern times when we go through hardship or sin, we expect some amazing experience of God's forgiveness, love and healing, and actually fail to bring our weakness and pain

[6] C.S. Lewis, *The Voyage of the Dawn Treader*, Fontana Lions.

as an offering; a sacrifice in humility before our Maker.

As I began to lay down that sacrifice, so God started to reveal the goodness and purpose in my life. Later, when I read Isaiah 58:8-11, God spoke of healing, restoration and new life, of how rightness, justice and a right relationship with Him would go before me, conducting me to peace and prosperity. *Then you shall call, and the Lord will answer; you shall cry, and He will say, Here I am* (Isaiah 58:9a, The Amplified Bible).

It showed what God wanted to do for me, then went on to give practical implications, saying that if I pour out that with which I sustain my own life to the needy, then shall my light arise in darkness and God will continually guide and satisfy in dry places.

Those words provided a beautiful meaning to suffering and brought with them the end of Spring Harvest. My time there had proved to be a journey; a journey of understanding that had led me through both the arid and dusty desert and into pastures green, where I had grazed and fed and been sustained.

Being near Easter I felt it was right to spend time thinking on the immeasurable suffering of Jesus because it would enable me to get my own suffering into perspective. I felt too that God was telling me I had not fought agonisingly against my pain or my sin of possessiveness and jealously in relationships. He said, 'There is a point to come where, in sheer agony, you will cry out to me and pour out your own blood.'

A few weeks later I found myself, as predicted, fighting agonisingly against the pain and depression, and pouring out my own blood in the language of tears. In my diary I wrote:

I wept like my body has *never* known me to weep before, with an anguish of heart that was beyond imagination. Such agony has brought me very close to the Lord and revealed the might of His Fatherhood and immeasurable compassion. Nothing can *ever* shake my faith now. How much God has revealed Himself to me of late. The depth of all that He is teaching me would never have been possible without the crumbling of the old clay. And how I praise Him for the deep roots He is causing me to lay down.

What was born out of that time was a deep, deep compassion. A compassion for God and for others; a compassion that made me smile inside.

I began to see that love is the key to all things. A love that is costly; a love that involves being pierced and the wearing of a crown of thorns, and forgiveness; a love that means suffering open wounds, but out of which will flow the fruits of the Spirit: love, joy, peace, patience, kindness, goodness, faithfulness, humility and self-control.

One Sunday I removed myself from the service at Greyfriars and sat alone behind the church on a broken brick wall. I spent an hour in prayer, praising God, coming in repentance for ways I had reacted, offering my forgiveness to those who had scarred me in the past, praying for close friends and asking to know God's touch. As my body drank in the warm sun, so my heart drank in the love of the Lord. I entered a time of deep worship, something that would not have been possible had I not learnt how to worship in brokenness. As the minutes passed I slid from pain to praise, to love, and was conscious of a deep peace.

On reading Philippians a short while later, it struck me that Paul not only carried in his heart a tremendous love for the people, but a great joy – a joy apart from circumstances. My prayer for my life is that my knowledge of that joy may continue to grow – not a euphoric joy, but a joy from within which is based on love and peace – a gift from God.

9

The rat race

So you work from nine to five
or eight to four.
If you are really unlucky
you work some more.

Then as your work day
comes to its end
you dash into town and
have a good spend.

There's all you need at
your finger tips,
from fashionable clothes
to burgers and chips.

When you've had enough
of the busy street
you stagger home
to rest your feet.

Then of course you socialise
if given the chance
discos, movies
or dinner and dance.

Life can be fun but each
day much the same,
little hope of adventure
or claim to fame.

There has to be more to life
than living like this.
Why not find out – give
the rat race a miss.

Still sitting on the plane from Nairobi to Johannesburg, I let my mind wander from the pain and challenges I had endured in the first few years after *Puppet on a String* was published to some of the lighter moments, such as leaving home in my late teens and the different places I had lived. My first accommodation I found through an advertisement in the local paper. I didn't know the outskirts of Reading very well and certainly not well enough to know that the bed-sit was in a very seedy area where there were more foreigners than English folk and all the local shops offered was Indian food. It was just as well that my taste buds relished the hot and spicy! The landlord showed me in: there were about five bed-sits inside the house, mine was on the first floor, next to the bathroom which we all shared. I couldn't wait to paint the room and decorate it to my own taste; it was the first time I'd had the opportunity to use my creativity in such a way.

I have to admit that the novelty of a place of my own did not last more than a few weeks when I discovered that I was the only girl amongst a handful of tough middle-aged men living off the State and earning cash-in-hand at the same time. They might not have been too nice with each other, but they were always pleasant enough to me, and were forever offering what they considered to be very useful advice – like how to fiddle the electricity meters, or how to smuggle gold out of Arab countries!

Coming in late at night never ceased to be a source of entertainment, especially when in the pitch-black my hand would fumble around trying to flick the light switch only to discover that yet again one of the men had taken the bulb in the hallway for his own use. I would then creep in the dark to the stairs to find that, strangely enough, the landing light didn't seem to work either! I soon got used to mountaineering in the dark and after a while also learnt how to find the keyhole of my door without first scraping half the paint off with the key!

I may have eventually got used to dark and eerie passages, but stumbling over a body in the night always took me by surprise. It was nothing unusual for one of the men to come home paralytic and collapse in a drunken stupor on the landing floor. A trip to the bathroom in the middle of the night could result in my being sent flying into blackness before I had the chance to pull the light switch to see what was there!

The blokes liked me because I asked the landlord to put in a pay-phone. The reason I proved to be popular was that they would then arrange for their friends to make reverse charge calls and the landlord would have to foot the bill! That soon put an end to the phone.

I shall never forget coming home one evening and opening the front door to be greeted by an angry voice and a large kitchen knife: one of the men had locked himself out of his room and thought the easiest way to get inside was to hack down the door! We stood and had a quick chat and then I thought I had better leave him to it and retreat to the safety of my own room!

I lasted eight months there. My next accommodation was quite different. Word had got around that I was looking for somewhere to live and in no time I received a phone call from someone at Henley Baptist Church. Two Christian girls were sharing a house in Caversham (a better part of Reading) and they needed a third. I found myself with a large room overlooking a green and living with Maggie, a teacher, Jane a nurse and Pussy-babe, an eccentric and lovable tabby cat.

Living in such 'ordinary' accommodation did not provide quite so many entertainments, but I can't say I was sorry about that! For most of the time I struggled to keep up with Maggie's social life, dashing frantically between Henley and Reading; dinner parties, coffee, chat, and Trivial Pursuit; swimming and the occasional disco on a cruise boat up the Thames on a balmy evening. Probably the most entertaining time was when Maggie, Jane and I had all been out for the evening; Jane and I went home early, as we both had to rise at an unsociable hour in the morning, leaving Maggie to enjoy herself. Having been fast asleep in bed for a few hours the next thing I was conscious of was the sound of smashing glass. My heart began to beat rapidly. I did not relish the thought of tackling intruders. It was Maggie. She had left her keys behind and did not want to wake us, so decided to remove the kitchen window pane, only it smashed in the process!

Besides all the more usual activities such as cycling, dancing, painting and reading, much of my social life and relaxation involved children. I have always loved children, which proved itself through my work as a crèche assistant and, later, as a nanny. It really helped to unwind to visit people like Ro, her husband Robin, and their two children Richenda and Alastair. I would hardly have set foot in the door before the children were dragging me into some activity – computer games, roller-blades, Technical Lego, or more likely, reading a chapter or two from one of Roald Dahl's books such as *George's Marvellous Medicine*. The only problem with so easily getting wrapped up in children's activities was that it left people uncertain as to where I stood in terms of the child/adult world (I wasn't sure myself either, as part of me felt more like a child). In my first year of knowing Richenda and Alastair they would frequently ask questions like, 'When you grow up do you want to be a dancer?'

To which I would have to reply, 'I already am grown up.'

With very serious faces they would say, 'Oh! Are you?'

Work and play were all very well, but my whole life seemed to revolve around Greyfriars Church, Reading, corporation buses and chain-stores. I was also finding that I was in constant demand to help eating disorder sufferers, give radio interviews or talks, which was becoming increasingly stressful. I was young and single and needed to experience life, so decided to think seriously about making a move and doing something different.

In answer to a cry one day of, 'What *shall* I do?', a friend thrust a piece of paper in my hand with the name and address of a missionary doctor who had been a GP in the UK and who for the past twenty-five years had worked in medicine and psychiatry in Southern Africa, Dr Guy Daynes. The friend was a medical student who herself had wanted to take up a volunteer post with Guy but who was unable to due to glandular fever. Not at all sure that he would take me on, because of my lack of medical experience, I wrote to enquire.

It had been such an 'on the spur of the moment' decision that to my shame I realised that I had not even prayed about it. I sat down and asked God to open and close doors accordingly. I would need a *very* definite sign that it was right to go.

The next day I was due to speak in Tonbridge at my first literary luncheon. Since I was bound to be talking and praying with sufferers afterwards and was asked to give a talk at a church in the evening, and would have had a long and tiring day, I accepted an invitation to stay the night and attend a Fisherfolk concert the following evening.

To my amazement soon after the concert had started

the Fisherfolk explained that much of their music would be different from usual as they had not long returned from a visit to South Africa. The African music, along with the culture and troubles out there, had had a big effect on them and influenced the style of their music and lyrics on their latest album, 'A Larger Place'. They went on to talk a little about South Africa and chose to sing a couple of the songs in Zulu. I laughed to myself and thought, 'Are you trying to tell me something Lord?'

It was well over a month before I received word from Guy, the psychiatrist in South Africa, and his wife, Jan, by which time I had virtually given up hope of going; yet I was becoming more and more convinced that it was South Africa to which God was calling me.

As usual, as soon as I heard the postman pushing the mail through the box, I rushed downstairs and thumbed through to see if there was anything for me. Noticing an airmail envelope with South African stamps on it, I hoped and prayed it was the news for which I had been waiting. I ripped open the envelope in eager anticipation.

My dear Helena,

Many thanks for your letter dated 16th April, and for your book, which have only just arrived. Having considered it, both Jan and I feel that the Lord has sent you to us, we will be pleased to have you on a voluntary basis for 6-12 months depending on how you enjoy being with us.

The job will primarily be as my research assistant which will involve recording specific patients who come within my research interest …

He went on to mention the three main conditions that he would be working on, post-natal depression, schizophrenia, and the role of alcohol intake in the causation of mental illness. He said that additional work could involve me in helping their psychiatric patients to paint, draw and dance as part of their therapy, and that I was welcome to come to South Africa any time after 20th June to suit my convenience.

The nature of the work that he mentioned in the letter was different from what I had been led to believe. The reason was that after twenty-five years he was leaving Transkei and moving to Madadeni Hospital, Newcastle, in Natal. The change in work and location suited me better, which in itself was confirmation that it was right to go. I could not believe how relaxed and at peace I was. Normally I would have been worrying and wanting to back out at the last minute. I wrote in my diary:

> God never ceases to amaze me; even in this short space of time He has given me signs that it is right to go to South Africa and that He will prepare me and equip me. I feel sure that He has something really incredible in store and that I am going to gain so much through this experience. I have never been so sure about a job or trip being right as I am about this one. I just know that this is where I am meant to go and I am sure that He will have everything worked out by the time I leave. It's really exciting!

Jan had added a note at the end of Guy's letter to say she was coming to England to visit family in a couple of months and that if I wanted to talk further about going to South Africa I must feel free to arrange to meet her.

When she arrived, I phoned Jan and we spent several very valuable hours together at her daughter's home in London. Out came the map of South Africa; I had no idea what South Africa was like as a country, of its size, or even much about the different cultures. I was incredibly ignorant; I knew little other than South Africa was connected to the word apartheid and that almost every night a report of another outburst of violence appeared on the news. I decided that as soon as I had finished talking with Jan I had better lay my hands on as many books about South Africa as possible and spend my spare time reading! Besides enlightening me with regard to culture, conditions and politics of the country, Jan passed on practical information concerning finance, clothing and travel. As she spoke the reality of my going began to sink in. Just before I left her she said,

'So are you going to join us?'

'Definitely,' I replied.

Now I was committed!

As soon as I said goodbye to Jan my toes began to twitch. The thought of Africa might have been somewhat daunting, but the excitement of taking on such a challenge was very great. I contacted USPG Missionary Society to see if there was any chance of sponsorship.

A few weeks later USPG called me to London for an interview. What came out of the next hour or two was further confirmation that it was right for me to go to South Africa. Without a second interview I was accepted as an Experience Exchange Student and given an exceptionally generous sponsorship. Two thirds of my airfare and insurance had been covered, a further third was still needed. Private individuals and my youth group, Crossroads, kindly gave donations. Only a matter of weeks before I was due to leave I still needed nearly two hundred pounds, but I was not sure how to tell everyone. Only a few days later I heard that Greyfriars Missionary Committee had agreed to give USPG two hundred pounds for me. By the time I was due to leave for Africa all expenses had been covered, down to the last penny.

One of the hardest things about knowing that it was South Africa to which I was going to go was waking up every morning to be reminded by the media that it is a troubled land. It was very easy to become negative and dwell only on the bad side that was constantly being portrayed. I would sit and wonder just how much of the violence, pain and conflict I would be likely to come across. At such times I would find myself saying, 'Why South Africa Lord? Why can't I go and work in, say, East Africa or India?'

Just as I had completely come to terms with the fact that South Africa was definitely the right place, I would bump into other people who would instil the negative into me again.

'I hear you're going to South Africa,' they would say.

'Yes, that's right,' I would reply, smiling all over.

'Do you think it's really safe to work there, I mean considering all the trouble? Why South Africa, why not India or Kenya or somewhere a little more stable?'

With that I would start asking myself questions like, 'It's true, how do I know that I'm going to be safe?' The only answer was to pray about it. I did just that and then felt called to read Psalm 91. I had never read it before but in doing so it was confirmation enough that despite any dangers I would be kept safe.

(God Our Protector)
Whoever goes to the LORD for safety,
Whoever remains under
the protection of the Almighty,
can say to him,
'You are my defender and protector.
You are my God; in you I trust'
He will keep you safe from all hidden dangers
and from all deadly diseases.
He will cover you with his wings;
you will be safe in his care;
his faithfulness will protect and defend you.
You need not fear any dangers at night
or sudden attacks during the day
or the plagues that strike in the dark
or the evils that kill in daylight.
A thousand may fall dead beside you,

ten thousand all around you,
but you will not be harmed.
You will look and see
how the wicked are punished.
You have made the LORD your defender,
the Most High your protector,
and so no disaster will strike you,
no violence will come near your home.
God will put his angels in charge of you
to protect you wherever you go.
They will hold you up with their hands
to keep you from hurting your feet on the stones.
You will trample down lions and snakes,
fierce lions and poisonous snakes.
God says, 'I will save those who love me
and will protect those who
acknowledge me as LORD.
When they call to me, I will answer them;
When they are in trouble, I will be with them.
I will rescue them and honour them.
I will reward them with long life;
I will save them.'

(GNB)

No words could have provided greater comfort or assurance or protection, and just to make sure that I had received the message someone else had also been given Psalm 91 for me. I had been invited to spend the evening with a missionary, home on furlough from Africa. Shortly before I left he said that earlier in the day he had been reading the Bible and God pointed him to two Psalms, one was Psalm 91. He said he hoped both Psalms would be meaningful but he felt that it was Psalm 91 that was particularly relevant for me. So right!

At peace and calmed about the whole experience, all that remained was for me actually to set foot in South Africa and feel it for real!

10

South of the Kalahari

South of the Kalahari
lies a land more
beautiful in parts
than I have ever seen.
A land of rich green
mountain slopes
and crystal waterfalls;
of lashing waves
and silky sand.
A land where the sun
sinks like liquid gold
and skies turn fiery red.

South of the Kalahari
lies a land more
beautiful in parts
than I have ever seen,
But a land sadly split
by 'apartheid'
and all that word suggests;
of searching hearts
and questioning minds.
A land where violence is
too often known and people
wonder what the future holds.

My mind had been so transported to the events of the past few years that I took in nothing of the scenery on the flight from Nairobi to Johannesburg, and was standing on South African soil before the reality of where I was going had even started to sink in. It was 1986 and I was setting foot alone in a very troubled land (1986 was the year that the General State of Emergency was called).

Jan was at the airport and stood out as a familiar face amongst the crowds, ready to help load the luggage into the car and undertake the four-hour drive to Newcastle. It was still Africa and yet so very different from Kenya. Throughout the journey I gazed at the countryside, trying to soak up the atmosphere of my new surroundings. Passing out of the Transvaal and into Natal we drove for miles without seeing a town, with nothing other than a vast expanse of veld and the rugged mountains in the distance breaking the horizon.

There were new noises, new smells and different lighting; a glow of beautiful gold was cast upon the land. Nearing Newcastle we wound our way along miles of twisting road amongst interesting vegetation, and I knew that it wouldn't take much for South Africa to captivate my heart. My first impression of Newcastle itself was terrible: a mining town which seemed to have little attraction and I wondered how on earth I would survive living there. Later I discovered that I had seen the worst part and that mostly it wasn't as bad! Apartheid was rampant in South Africa, with Newcastle being a 'white' town, with living areas for the 'coloureds' and 'Indians', and it was as we approached it that I learnt that the hospital campus on which I would be living was sixteen kilometres away in the 'black' township of Madadeni.

We drove on across yet more veld to the edge of the township, past dozens of small brick houses, tightly packed together, all with twisted corrugated iron roofs. A few larger and more elaborate houses contrasted with the many scruffy-looking little shacks. Cows, goats and chickens wandered aimlessly by the roadside and dust fogged up the car windscreen. A fence of barbed wire surrounded the rehabilitation centre for alcoholics and drug addicts, and only a short distance on we came to yet more barbed wire; knotted and about three feet thick the wire defined the edge of the hospital campus with a clear message of 'keep out'. The guard on duty opened the gates for us and as we bumped over the cattle grid Jan raised her hand and shouted, 'Siabonga' – my first Zulu word – 'thank you'.

The campus seemed pleasant enough – a collection of about fifteen houses, all single-storey, as is most common in South Africa, with the exception of Guy and Jan's house which towered above the others with its double layer, signifying Guy's significance. All the houses were uniformly built of brick, had corrugated iron roofs, walled courtyards and open-plan gardens. All around were plants and vegetables of every kind, prickly pears, bamboos, grapevines, lemon trees and a profusion of flowers. In the distance stood majestic mountains, their blue hue merging with the cloudless sky.

As we walked into the house I could hear the television spouting Afrikaans, yet another language which sounded double Dutch to me. Guy stepped forward with a warm welcome; a rosy complexion, white hair and quite an air of mischief about him – not an image I held of a psychiatrist at all, much to my relief! He handed me the pile of mail which had accumulated over the weeks and I was shown my room, which was basic but spacious and looked out across grass and trees towards the hospital and township beyond.

All evening I was aware of new sounds and lay awake in bed tossing and turning. Dogs barked outside, not one or two but what sounded like forty or fifty. Thunder crashed, lightning dazzled and rain beat upon the metal roof outside my window. It was one of many storms which were to follow in the next few weeks and I thought of what my friend Joan had written in a card for me shortly before leaving England.

> I am so glad that the Lord you have met, known and loved here is going with you to South Africa. Everything else will be new and strange and exciting but the abiding thing is His love. He is in you, around you, over you and before you – there is no situation that can take Him by surprise.

I had the weekend to adjust, unpack and gain some kind of order in my life before becoming heavily involved in work. First on the agenda was a guided tour of the hospital, a single-storey brick building with apparently the longest hospital corridor in Southern Africa – two kilometres! Jan led the way across the campus, through a hole in the fence and across a field, where so many feet had passed that a sandy track had been worn in the grass. There in front of us stood the entrance to the hospital. It was a Zulu Government Hospital and it was only Zulus that would be found there.

The first section we came to was the outpatients' department. Crowds of people with hot steamy bodies were sitting talking or wandering up and down restlessly, waiting to receive attention. Many raised their hands and passed their greetings of 'Sanibona'. It didn't take long to see that the Zulus are a very friendly people. Battling our way through the mass of needy people we passed the plaster room, disaster room and theatre, before turning the corner towards the intensive care unit and physiotherapy department and around another corner towards the general wards. We had only just started our visit and I was already beginning to wonder if I would ever find my way around this rabbit warren of a hospital alone!

The first ward we entered was the children's surgical – one of the three children's wards in which it was hoped I would run regular play therapy sessions. It was different from the well-equipped, clean, orderly hospitals I had been used to in England. The wards were bare; there were no toys and no pictures, just little sorrowful black bodies sitting or lying on crumpled sheets, looking somewhat bemused, their large brown eyes staring into space. The younger children were dressed in simple white cotton gowns which were tied at the back and the older ones were wearing khaki or blue shorts and tops. My heart went out to them. How I longed to spend time encouraging and stimulating them.

Besides the surgical wards there were the medical and TB wards, the occupational therapy department and the psychiatric side of the hospital to visit too. In total there were 1,600 beds, not to mention outpatients! Between wards lay attractive little gardens, full of rose bushes and hibiscus flowers, in which several of the psychiatric patients were working hard at keeping them well weeded, whilst other patients had given up on the job and lay in groups, like sacks of potatoes, on the grass – their khaki uniforms fading beneath the blazing beams of the midday sun.

By the end of the morning it was a relief to see the large hall and teaching block knowing that open space lay just beyond. Fresh air – what a relief! I had never much liked hospitals, so why I had ended up working in one, goodness knows!

It took me the best part of my first month at Madadeni to become properly acquainted with the hospital, feel confident and know all the short cuts. Most of my first months there were spent working with the children. Firstly sorting out the vast number of toys donated by local white schools, washing them, marking them with a large ZG (Zulu Government), and distributing them amongst the children, secondly building up regular play therapy sessions on the different wards.

When I first approached the children they seemed sceptical, suspicious of my motive and unsure how to respond. I reached for a bundle of toys and passed them to the group of youngsters sitting close by me; vacant eyes stared. Many of them had not seen toys such as these before – books, dolls, puzzles – and they didn't know what to do with them. Gently I moved a little closer and showed them what play was all about; I could not explain in words; language was a barrier, as they did not understand English and it would be a long time before I could speak enough Zulu, so communication was limited to actions, signs and facial expression!

The first few weeks brought about little other than sheer frustration. The toys I had spent hours mending and marking lay in pieces, broken on the floor, or had disappeared altogether – slipped into the bag of a discharged patient. Books which I had carefully bound became piles of shredded paper, pictures which I had helped the children to paint were torn and hanging off the walls and nursing staff seemed unable to explain the whereabouts of even quite cumbersome toys or to give any idea which of the patients, parents or staff had a tendency to be light-fingered! Through bitter experience I learnt that you never leave wax crayons behind, even with the older children, otherwise the entire ward becomes a colourful creation, and you certainly don't stick pictures on the wall below arm's reach from a cot.

I discovered that a shady corner outside was a better place than any to hold the play therapy sessions. Away from ward walls and not under anyone's feet, the children had space enough in the brick courtyards to create. We mostly played ball games or sat and painted, trying hard to keep the paint on the paper, even if sometimes fingernails and toenails and faces came away a shade more decorative than before! The children laughed and smiled and their once sad little faces beamed with radiance and life, such warmth melting away any evidence of pain and suffering. It didn't take long for me to win their acceptance or for their enthusiasm to grow. I only had to appear round the ward door with a box bulging with brushes, paints and paper, and a ball tucked under my arm, and loud applause would burst forth, little feet would scamper in my direction, gather around and then follow me out into the fresh air, as though this was an enactment of the Pied Piper.

It was rewarding for me to watch the change. There was no comparison between their initial response – that of suspicion and empty eyes – and later their cheering and laughter and desperate rush for the 'goodies' in my box. After we had finished painting and I had convinced them as best I could in my broken ten-word Zulu that it was time to leave, they would drag me into the ward and individually point to the patch of wall above their beds. It was important that the right picture went above the right bed so that at visiting hours there was plenty of scope for pride.

At the end of the day, having spent time on two or three wards, working with the older children and giving much needed TLC (tender loving care) to the younger ones, I would head for home. Nearly always several of the children would follow me out of the wards, chattering amongst themselves, up to the end of the corridor, where they would stop and wave goodbye, watching me disappear into the sinking sun. I turned and smiled; a little wave meant 'I'll see you again soon'. Clutching my box of dirty brushes, empty paint pots and any acquired broken toys, it was out of the brick maze into the heat, across the grassy field, through the hole in the fence and along what had commonly become known as 'fly-path'. Dozens of flies would bombard me; some even had the audacity to use my nose as a runway, my eyes as a bath and my ears as dance floors. I would start shaking my head vigorously and throwing my body from side to side, then to my horror would realise that my strange movements were visible to the world and I would turn a deep shade of pink and make a hurried dash for the cover of the trees.

The hours I spent with the children became fewer by the week, not by choice but because of the need for greater involvement in other areas of work. The addition of two extremely capable and enthusiastic occupational therapists made it easy for me quietly to slip away, although my heart was too deeply involved in the very lives and nature of the children not to visit them at least once a week.

One of my new projects took me over to the psychiatric section of the hospital. I was asked to paint murals on the walls of wards for children and adults with severe learning disabilities and associated conditions in an effort to brighten them up and provide some form of stimulation for the children. My first assignment was on the most severe ward. I was unsure what to expect. As I opened the brightly coloured door, my initial reaction was to walk away; the sight, smells and sounds which lived within those four walls brought about an intense revulsion. There were grossly malformed children, some unable to talk or walk or control themselves, some making noises difficult to accept as being human. The hot, sticky environment intensified the worst of the smells and at times it was so overpowering that feelings of nausea welled up.

The walls had recently been painted in a nondescript cream colour, which gave me a smooth and easy background to work on. I came to the conclusion that any art work must be well out of fingers' reach and so my priority had to be to pay a visit to the workshop and obtain a ladder.

The murals required a reasonable amount of concentration and stretching of limbs in peculiar positions to achieve exactly what I wanted. The trouble came in putting too much concentration into what I was painting and not enough into where I was standing. One day when leaning into the corner of the room on the top of a ladder I came crashing down six feet on to concrete. I hit the ground with force and lay stunned on my side. I was in so much pain that if I had not laughed at my stupidity I would have screamed loudly enough for the whole hospital to hear! I didn't break my arm as I thought, but suspected I had broken ribs and later discovered a clot. But I survived.

Falling off ladders was one thing, being pulled off was another. The second ward I worked on was still considered a children's ward because of the mental state of the patients but there was no mistaking that physically they were mature women. Most of them were at least twice my size too, which had its problems when I was up the ladder and they decided to pull at my legs for attention or walk off with one of my paint pots. I found myself in a constant state of racing up and down ladders to rescue vital pieces of equipment and trying not to sound too annoyed lest I should become an innocent victim of their muscles! Their being bigger and stronger and more apt to wander also meant that everything was under lock and key and I frequently found myself locked in with the less manageable patients. This experience was not exactly welcome, especially when at the end of the day I had to go against my introverted nature and bellow through the key hole to be released!

However frustrating the practicalities of painting the murals were, nevertheless I considered all my effort worthwhile when the nurses started telling me how much they and the children appreciated the pictures, although one of the children was somewhat perplexed when I had drawn and painted a hare and not yet put in the eyes. He turned to the nurse, covered his eyes with his hands and moved his arms and legs about as if to say, 'How can a hare run without eyes?' What a stupid artist!

It felt wonderful to be in the rural African atmosphere, away from the humdrum of hectic UK city life. Wonderful too to be away from the demands which so quickly fell upon me to help eating disorder sufferers after writing *Puppet on a String*. Once a fortnight I spent an extra hour or so in Psychiatry with Guy, taking patient histories and assisting him with his research. He assured me he'd not come across a case of anorexia in his twenty-six years of working in rural African hospitals and I was pleased! It felt good to be learning of other conditions: schizophrenia was a new and fascinating phenomenon for me.

Each lunchtime Guy, Jan and I would meet back at the house and sit down to eat, quite formally. We would catch up on our morning's work before a short rest and Guy's and my return to different parts of the hospital. One particular lunchtime Guy shared how he had seen a patient that morning that he would like me to see with him. He was sure it was anorexia and he wanted a second opinion. We returned to his consulting room. The young girl was the first case of anorexia he had stumbled across in his twenty-six years and it so happened I was there that year! The result was that I was given a psychi-atrist's consulting room, was called 'doctor' by the nursing staff (who knew no different) and was told to get on with the job! I sat down in the large swivel chair, spun myself around a few times, read through the case notes and then called in my patient! Some challenge! I had counselled a number of anorexics before, but never with the use of an interpreter. It made my job twice as hard!

Lila was a seventeen-year-old Zulu and a classic case of anorexia nervosa with vomiting. When I first saw her she had been hospitalised in Zululand for several weeks and had managed to pick up some weight, but was still terribly emaciated.

What went against the 'rules' of anorexia was that Lila was not white, she had not been dieting and she did not come from an affluent society. She had been brought up in a rural township in Zululand where such luxuries as running water and electricity are not known. Her mother was only earning R23 (approximately £8) a week, which had to cover feeding her five children. The father no longer supported the family as he was not married to Lila's mother, claiming he could not afford the wedding price (a certain number of cattle) requested by the mother's family. Consequently Lila's mother could not afford a home of her own and had to resort to renting a room in someone else's home with one of her children; the rest of the children, including Lila, had been distributed amongst relatives.

Slowly the frustration and pain that Lila had experienced over the years was revealed: the feeling of rejection, wanting to be with her mother, and many other deep feelings. The circumstances surrounding her illness might have been very different from 'affluent white' anorexia, but the symptoms remained the same, even to the extent of lack of self-acceptance and perfectionism. Culturally things were very different too; the regarding of illness as an evil spirit, the involvement of the witch doctor and the means of expressing and understanding of feelings.

Gradually, after many hours of discussion and working through some of the difficulties, Lila started to look more healthy and happy and to gain some confidence. At the end of each consultation I would take her into Guy's office so that he could assess the situation. He too was pleased with her progress and after several months she was discharged from the hospital in Zululand and from outpatients at Madadeni. Years later I heard that she had made a lasting recovery.

In addition to spending time in Psychiatry and writing up and illustrating lecture notes on overhead projector transparencies for Guy, the need had arisen to spend several hours each week at the rehabilitation centre for alcoholics and drug addicts. The 'rehab', as it was most commonly called, consisted of a nicely-designed brick building surrounded by barbed wire and situated in the township. It housed both men and women, and the majority of the patients had been committed there because of involvement in some criminal offence. Many seemed to be reasonably intelligent and well educated, and until the point of their addiction they had held good jobs, and therefore could speak or at least understand English.

I had been asked if I would take exercise classes with the patients two or three mornings a week. Until a few months previously they had had extremely unadventurous and lifeless relaxation exercises which were enough to send them from 'rehab' to 'psychi'!

When Jan was not going over by car, getting to the 'rehab' involved walking out of the hospital gates and going along a dusty road through the township. More than once I had a close encounter with a group of goats and cows which quite obviously considered me an intruder on their territory, but fortunately had the decency to let me pass unscathed and to take the exercise class with the patients. Little did I realise at the time that actually the animals should have been the least of my worries. The reality was that I was a young white woman walking alone through the dusty paths of a black township in the height of the apartheid regime.

The first time I took the exercise class I felt completely overwhelmed. I bounced up to the hall a bundle of energy, tape recorder and music tucked under my arm, and flung open the door only to stumble over a pile of lethargic bodies! These were the 'unenthusiastic inmates' who refused to comply with the rules of compulsory morning prayers, exercise classes or the carrying out of daily duties. At least some of the patients were enthusiastic and threw their arms and legs in all directions in time with the music. By the end of the half-hour I was relieved to escape the smell of hot sweaty bodies and have the chance to relax in the superintendent's office with a much needed cup of coffee.

The exercise classes kept me not only fit but amused too. One morning I was a little late arriving and as I walked down the corridor I could hear that the patients had started without me. When I opened the door, to my horror, I discovered that the self-appointed 'instructor' was forcing them to do very deep breathing exercises and they were falling to the ground like swatted flies!

Seeing the need in the patients for relaxation, affirmation and the gaining of self-worth, I asked if it would be possible for me to start an art therapy class; an informal few hours when the patients could come and go as they pleased and there would be scope for enjoyment, expression of feelings, social chat or deeper talk as the need arose. Once I had acquired the materials, I was given the freedom of the dining room in which to work, a very large and airy room with plenty of windows and the nearest to a school art room I would ever find. The social worker spread word around amongst the patients he felt would be interested that the class was in operation and on the first day two or three extremely unartistic men turned up, one of whom became very frustrated with his lack of achievement and swore he would never return.

The class carried on along similar lines for a number of

weeks, never more than about four people and a distinct lack of enthusiasm. I was just about to give it up when things looked up, the numbers started to increase, women as well as men rolled up and I stumbled across two very talented artists. Within a short space of time I had a regular attendance of between twelve and fifteen enthusiastic patients who were asking if it would be possible to have a twice-weekly instead of once-weekly class!

I would sit patiently watching them paint scenes from their everyday life and tribal traditions or express their feelings in art form. Some of the pictures were very expressive, speaking of the misery of alcohol addiction; the anger, resentment, hostility, helplessness and fruit-lessness of their situation. Often they showed the battle that they were in; wanting to get better and yet feeling powerless to do so. Just sitting back and looking, I realised how very different these people were from me; in their circumstances, living conditions, cultures and traditions. Yet I could fully identify with the fight and such differences as existed did not prevent communication and relaxed atmosphere. We had our moments of silence and our moments of laughter and as one week faded into another so my understanding of these people grew, not just as 'black South Africans', Zulus or any other tribe, but as alcoholics and drug addicts and more important as individuals. I felt privileged to have the opportunity of working with them and of helping them gain a little pleasure during this self-destructive and self-hating phase of their lives. It was always sad when one of the group had come to the end of his time at 'rehab' and had to leave; sad in some ways but a time for rejoicing too because it meant he had progressed suffi-ciently to be allowed home – unless he had absconded, as was the case with one of my best artists!

11

To laugh and cry

We are born
to laugh and cry;
to be glad when
others are glad
and weep with
those who are sad.

We are born
to feel some
of the world's
deepest pain
then relax and
relieve the strain.

We are born
to know the
joys of receiving
and giving;
the heights and
depths of living.

We are born
for tears and smiles
and neither
should deny
for to live and love
is to laugh and cry.

Working for Guy proved varied and interesting, creating opportunities which I would never have been given in England. One such occasion was helping him at a medical congress in Johannesburg, where he was to present a poster-session on mental illness after child-birth, talking about seven clinically recognisable disorders.

Once at the congress my job was to assist Guy at the poster-session, but otherwise I had plenty of time to attend seminars, talk to doctors and go to social functions. I was supposed to be attending the women's programme where lectures were far more low-key, but I found it more stimulating to go to lectures for the GPs where I could enjoy hearing about such things as psychotherapeutic counselling skills.

Most eventful and exhausting of all was my second day in Johannesburg. I was picked up early in the morning by the South African section of my publishers, Hodder and Stoughton, and whisked off to SABC (South African Broadcasting Corporation) for two radio interviews and a television interview. Technically everything conceivable went wrong with the television interview and I was kept on tenterhooks for well over an hour before the interview could start. By lunchtime I had arrived back at the hotel in time for a lecture for the ladies on adolescent problems. Part-way through I was taken completely unawares and asked to speak on anorexia.

The following couple of hours were spent speaking with a doctor from England who has been using my book *Puppet on a String* as a means of therapy with his patients. It was an interesting, if somewhat intensive, time.

By the end of our discussion my brain felt as if it had been on an assault course, and I was ready to sleep for twelve hours. Instead it was off to a restaurant for a quick curry. The heat of the curry soon woke me up and set me on my way for a one-and-a-half-hour session with the head psychiatrist from the medical school, who has a particular interest in anorexia. Unfortunately he was not the sort of person who took in everything you had to say and accepted it, but instead he loved to challenge. Hence I had a one-and-a-half-hour game of mental ping-pong, and felt as if every ounce of blood had been drained out of my body by the end!

The busy city life in Jo'burg was a contrast to the township life of Madadeni, to which I had become accustomed and whilst I had enjoyed my time there it was a relief to leave the sophisticated rat race for a simpler life style again.

Winter was beginning to settle in, many of the trees began to shed their leaves and the countryside started to take on its 'winter beige' look. Nights were incredibly cold. Sometimes in the morning there would be frost and ice on the bird tray, but days were often hot and we were blessed with cloudless blue skies and unbelievably beautiful sunsets.

My work continued to be as varied as the seasons. Besides additional roles at the hospital, I was becoming more and more involved in work at the church. I attended the local Anglican church in Newcastle, a multi-racial church some sixteen kilometres from the hospital campus. Guy and Jan were very active members of Holy Trinity and almost on my arrival they introduced me to Mike and Rosemary, the Rector and his wife. Within two or three weeks Rosemary had pronounced me a Sunday school teacher!

I grew to love working in the Sunday school and found the children enthusiastic and interesting. For quite a small church there was a very large Sunday school – there could be over a hundred children. I was responsible for the eleven and twelve year olds and on average would have between ten and fifteen children in my care. I was also fortunate in having the opportunity of getting to know some of my Sunday school pupils better when Rosemary and I restarted the junior youth group which had been dormant for some time.

My introduction to youth work in South Africa took place only a couple of weeks after I had arrived in the country when I was given the chance to participate in a course on leadership of youth being held by Africa Enterprise and Youth For Christ in Pietermaritzburg. It was fortunate that Rodney, the Youth Pastor of the Methodist church, was also going and could solve my problem of how to get there.

We set off early on the Friday morning to avoid the heat of the day and so that we could spend some time on the farm of a friend of Rodney's just outside Pietermaritzburg. The only mishap occurred as we were nearing the farm and quietly driving along a dirt road when suddenly the battery of his car caught fire. No problem! We pulled up the back seat which covered the battery, threw in a pile of sand and drove on! Still, it provided us with a few laughs and once at our destination we went on to enjoy a relaxing time swimming in the pool and sitting on the veranda drinking tea. Feeling greatly refreshed we made our way to the house where we were to stay and on to the AE centre to register. The centre, which is greatly concerned with reconciliation between black and white, and led by Michael Cassidy, is situated in beautiful surroundings.

The course proved very interesting and as well as

providing ideas and moral support it gave me valuable insight into the emotional and physical needs and attitudes, political and religious beliefs, peer pressure and motivation of the different groups that exist in South Africa – English-speaking White, Afrikaans-speaking White, Black, Coloured and Indian. All these I would come into contact with in my work at the hospital and church.

In addition to the main course I chose to do two electives. The first was on township crises, which proved essential for my work at Madadeni, giving valuable information on the reasoning behind the conflicts within the townships: the desire for one man, one vote and the longing for equality – equality in housing, education and opportunity. The second elective was on counselling. Much of the information I had already come across before but there was one area which was completely new to me, that of conscription, and being a youth leader in South Africa it would prove to be an unavoidable issue.

It was difficult for me to comprehend what it was like for white male South Africans leaving school or university being faced with two years in the army; being sent to the border to protect their country from invasion or having to go into the black townships and be faced with the possibility of being ordered to shoot people they might know and love. The alternative is for them to become conscientious objectors and be sent to prison for several years, or to leave the country for good. For some there is no trauma in facing their two years in the army or being called up for three months each year. For others the prospect is agony and one that can end in nervous breakdown. For those who become conscientious objectors, their decision may quite easily result in guilt and emotional conflict. There was much need for understanding and support, as I soon found out.

I was pleased too that the course provided time for meaningful worship, informal talk, reflection, fun and laughter. I came away from the three days not only over-heated, having sat through lectures in temperatures more suitable for frying eggs, but bubbling over with enthusiasm for work back at Holy Trinity.

A few months later my sudden burst of energy was channelled when Rosemary and I officially re-opened the junior youth group. We made a good pair. Rosemary took care of the devotions and I arranged and super-vised all the social and activity side of the afternoon. In no time we had a regular attendance each Friday of around twenty youngsters between the ages of nine and twelve. Most of them were Coloured, very lively and full of fun; their enthusiasm for the newly-formed group was proved by many of them walking several miles to reach the church hall whether in scorching sun or pelting rain.

I found the work enormously rewarding and looked forward to Friday afternoons, when I would cadge a lift into Newcastle with one of the doctors and prepare for the group. Some of the children would have already arrived half an hour early and be waiting outside the door in eager anticipation. More often than not they would use that half-hour conjuring up some trick to play on me and being my gullible, unsuspecting self I would walk straight into their play and cause fits of uncontrol-lable laughter!

Even the naughtiest and most rebellious of them proved loveable, and there were certainly one or two from broken and very sad backgrounds who could be extremely difficult to handle. Good and bad alike, they were all for action and would eagerly ask, in a profusion of jumbled words and contrasting voices, what we would be doing that afternoon before I had even had a chance to unlock the doors.

As if taking care of the junior youth group were not enough, I started running programmes for the teenagers, or occasionally I would join Rodney, at the Methodist church, who was managing about fifty young people single-handed.

Youth work took me to other parts of South Africa besides Newcastle. The leadership of youth course that I had attended brought about an invitation by Youth For Christ to return to Pietermaritzburg for a week to speak in schools and hostels as part of their outreach work. It proved to be an action-packed time with a great many opportunities to minister to youngsters both in large gatherings and on a one-to-one basis.

The climax of the week was the super rally organised by Youth For Christ and held in the City Hall. The room was overflowing with young people – well over a thousand of all colours and races. It was an evening of music, comedy, drama, talks, and above all, a time of reconciliation between the different cultural groups. There was plenty of scope for learning, teaching, giving and infilling, and the chance to meet new people. One of the contacts I made was with the Youth Worker at Prestbury Methodist church. Youth For Christ had arranged for me to stay with Carol during the latter part of the week and in that time we struck up a good friendship and she was already making arrangements for me to join her in a youth outreach programme later in the year.

Returning to Madadeni, after the week in Pietermaritzburg, I felt as if I were walking through the wilderness alone, ploughing a field of rock-solid ground. I spent much time questioning why the Lord had placed me in a situation where I was isolated from much Christian fellowship and did not often have the chance to socialise with people of my own age.

After crying out to God I read a passage in the book by Mother Basilea Schlink, *Father of Comfort*, which talked about the Father being the vine-dresser and the need for him to prune the vines in the first few years. Whilst it seems as though we are not bearing any fruit, we are in fact being prepared for greater fruitfulness. It was good to read such a passage and in time it brought about complete acceptance of the situation I was in and I realised that walking through the dry and barren land was going to teach me so much more than running through a field of golden corn.

Despite the frustrations and hard work involved in the youth groups I found it challenging and interesting working with the youngsters, not only because I love involvement in people's lives, but for the simple reason that the youth of today are the future generation and the hope for South Africa to come.

Before going to South Africa I had not the slightest interest in politics and had steered well clear of any discussion along those lines; I certainly did not see the prospect of going to a 'politically explosive' country as 'exciting', as people had suggested. In fact when I stepped onto South African territory I vowed I would never get involved. However, not to do so would have proved virtually impossible and wrong of me, especially when so-called politics affected the very hearts and lives of the people with whom I was working and socialising.

I began to see the complexity of the situation in South Africa and, whilst it was not in my nature to get actively involved, the situation always remained on my heart. I saw a country filled with a diversity of peoples – Blacks divided, Whites divided, Indians divided and Coloureds unsure of their own identity. I saw the pain which resulted from the Group Areas Act and the creation of second-class citizens; I saw the frustration and anger leading to faction fighting so that Blacks were fighting Blacks, terrorising townships, burning down schools, setting people alight; I saw mob violence spreading like fire, and the fleeing of the perpetrators before the police could arrive. I heard the declaration of the General State of Emergency and became aware of some of the devastating effects it would have on people's lives. I experienced the growing tensions in the township around

Soweto Day; watched the police and army out in force; and saw each house on the hospital campus being issued with buckets of sand in case of fire and witnessed the land around our houses set alight leaving the stretch between the houses and the hospital a field of black, stubbly grass. I saw two bouts of trouble take place in Madadeni and felt the pain of one, for a black friend of Jan's lost everything she owned when her house was set alight.

I saw and heard and felt a great deal during the months in South Africa and could understand the pain and difficulties from both black and white perspectives. Whilst there were times of encouraging evidence of change, such as hotels and other public places being opened to all races, as someone wisely pointed out to me, the abolition of petty apartheid makes no difference to the major social problems, and the division of people into tribes exacerbates the problems and gives Whites the opportunity to say that Blacks cannot be trusted with political power.

If there was one thing I soon realised, it was that there was no easy solution to the situation and yet that was no excuse for not working towards reconciliation.

It was in Christianity that I saw most barriers broken down and love, harmony and peace exist. Yet one could not ignore the distinct division within the Anglican Church; namely those who were for and those who were opposed to political involvement.

Mike, the Rector, and I would spend many a long hour discussing the frustration over the division as well as some of the difficulties that existed in being a multi-racial church.

Gradually we began to see encouraging changes and responses taking place at Holy Trinity, especially after a 'Partners in Mission' weekend which was a course specially designed to motivate reconciliation and growth within the church. The weekend seemed to help many people in very practical ways – in evangelism, prayer, meeting others' needs and generally being more effective Christians.

Often after an eventful day at the church I would not go back to Madadeni but spend the night with Mike and Rosemary who always had a bed made up for me, awaiting the arrival of their 'prodigal daughter'. Their two sons Kenneth and Robert were like younger brothers to me and they looked after a kitten of mine that I managed to adopt and name Jabulani (Zulu for happiness, rejoice)! Jabulani was a little bundle of black fur and was always around somewhere when I called, usually up to mischief, bringing 'itchy-balls' into the house and scattering them around. Vesta, the dog, was a real character, she loved Jabulani and often played with her – pinning her to the ground and rubbing her nose on Jabulani's tummy until there was a loud, 'Vesta, leave that kitty alone!' from everyone around.

Mike and Rosemary's home had always been open to me but it was when they invited me to go away with them on a long weekend that I really got to know them as a family. They took me to New Hanover, which had been their previous parish and was in the heart of the Natal countryside. It was the land of sugar cane and maize farming and we stayed with friends of theirs in a colonial-style farmhouse with enough bedrooms to start an orphanage and a sitting room the size of a ballroom! Their dog was the largest dog I have ever seen, even though it was still a puppy. Coming up beside it I felt distinctly like Alice in Wonderland after she had shrunk!

The days were carefree and I spent much of the time with Kenneth and Robert learning how to let go of my inhibitions and become a tomboy. If we weren't playing tennis or going for an early morning run, we were trying to catch a couple of very wild horses to ride or tearing through the sugar-cane fields over lumpy and muddy ground in a rattly old baakie (type of van). Many an hour we would sit quietly in the fields practising our shooting by firing at half-eaten mealie cobs or paper targets. The days were hot and we would sit chewing sugar-cane sticks for refreshment until it almost came out of our ears.

The evenings were warm and restful, the golden sun slowly sinking behind the sugar plantations. It was a time for social chat and unwinding after all the activity of the day.

It meant a great deal to me to spend time with a family and feel a part of their home and lives. It made a pleasant change too to step away from campus life for the occasional weekend.

12

Fun and friendship

Fun and friendship,
laughter filled days,
barbecues and fondues,
singing and praise.
These were some
of my happiest days.

Sea and sand,
huge lashing waves,
walking in mountains
and sleeping in caves.
These were some
of my happiest days.

Apart from work at the hospital and church, a demand for speaking on anorexia was also growing, and by the end of May I had spoken fifteen times in twelve weeks. That was as many times as I had spoken in England over a period of twelve months! Numbers attending increased too: I thought that three hundred at my second talk was unbelievable until I was faced with an audience of six hundred at my third talk! At least there was a genuine interest in what I had to say and it really came as no surprise to hear that anorexia is a big problem amongst the Whites in South Africa and for that very reason I found myself being asked to visit almost every school in Newcastle and surrounding areas in an attempt to reach the most vulnerable age group.

Besides schools I was also invited to speak at church gatherings and formal women's meetings, and asked to present a dual lecture to the nurses at Madadeni, with Guy, on eating disorders. Such an interest in the subject arose that I began to receive letters from various parts of South Africa asking if I would ever be in the area, and consequently Jan and I sat down and mapped out a speaking tour for my last month in the country.

I found public speaking and much of the work that I was involved in to be a draining experience, constantly in a position of giving out and with little chance of receiving back. Besides Guy and Jan there was only one other Christian in the doctors' quarters – Tammy, a Zulu doctor – and only a few weeks after I had got to know him, sadly he had to leave. There was no one my own age and I often felt devoid of Christian fellowship and thought of how I had taken for granted my church in England. I had been used to a couple of services each Sunday – young people's meetings, Bible studies, social evenings and always people around with whom to talk to and pray. The church at Newcastle was nice, but lacked the same vitality and even there I was in a constant state of giving out.

I could not deny the moments of isolation and frustration and it was in moments like these that I called out to God. At one such time I came across two passages in Mother Basilea Schlink's book, *Father of Comfort*.

> Keep your quiet times with God. Give Him more time. Abiding in God's presence cannot be replaced by anything. In the presence of God you will become strong. Through His presence you will be transformed. Seek His presence and it will solve everything that you cannot solve by yourself.
>
> There are three little words that contain the solution to all your problems. They are, 'Trust in God.' That means believing that God is really almighty and is really a Father full of love, always prepared to help. Trust and the first step towards the solution of your difficulties has been taken. The second will follow. With your own eyes you will see that in His time He will transform your sorrow into joy.[7]

Giving God more time and the keeping of quiet times was something that spoke to me very deeply. People from my area group at Greyfriars Church had prayed that I would have the ability to minister to myself, recognising that I would be devoid of fellowship, but I could not expect that

---

[7] Basilea Schlink, *Father of Comfort*, Lakeland.

ability unless I spent time in God's presence daily. Staying close to God is like a medicine healing all our wounds, quite apart from keeping life in perspective. I drew very close to God during the time in South Africa, partly because I was completely reliant on Him, rather than other people, and partly because I disciplined myself. I would wake up early in the morning, go for a thirty minute run around the campus and then come back to spend whatever time was left in a quiet time. It is true, abiding in God's presence cannot be replaced by anything and it was through His presence that I was transformed.

Occasionally opportunities arose for fellowship. Shortly before Tammy left the hospital he invited me to join him at an HCF (Hospital Christian Fellowship) meeting. I was the only white face amongst a sea of over a hundred black faces and was in for a new experience. Their meetings were very free and went on for as long as they felt like doing so, and their worship was spontaneous and full of joy. The Zulus are extremely gifted in their singing and able to harmonise from an early age. There was no need to have musical instruments – a handful of people could lift the roof off and keep perfectly in tune at the same time. They sang at every opportunity, often clapping their hands before anyone stood up to speak and after they had sat down again. It was customary for new people to walk to the front of the room, introduce themselves and speak for as long as they wished.

Tammy tapped me on the shoulder and told me to 'go forward'. It was totally against my timid nature but I walked to the front, greeted them all with the common greeting to which there was a loud response of 'Amen,' and I promptly went on to talk about the fact that I had come from England to work at Madadeni for a year and how privileged I felt to be able to join them at the meeting. When I had finished, there was another loud 'Amen' from all over the room and everyone burst into song. Most of the meeting was in Zulu, but it didn't seem to matter that I could not understand much; more important was the visual evidence of the deep, deep love that each one had for God and for one another.

After Tammy left I periodically went to the HCF meetings with Guy and Jan but my main form of fellowship and getting to know people was through a twenties-plus group at the Methodist church in Newcastle. Rodney, the Youth Pastor, had heard that an English girl working out at Madadeni was in need of young company and spiritual infilling, and only a few weeks after I had been in South Africa he came to visit me to ask if I would like to join his group. I used to look forward to Tuesday evenings enormously. I usually managed to cadge a lift with one of the doctors who lived in Newcastle and ask to be dropped off at Holy Trinity, the church I attended, where Mike and Rosemary, the Rector and his wife, would kindly feed me and make me feel at home whilst I waited for the tap on the back door announcing that Rodney had arrived to whisk me off to the meeting. The meetings were informal; usually only five or six of us gathered in a lounge for Bible study and coffee, or sometimes a social evening.

Amongst many other things I have fond memories of Chinese braais (barbecues), fondues and lots of laughter. Then at the end of the evening Rodney would safely deliver me back to Mike and Rosemary who always had a bed made up for me to sleep the night before making my way back to the hospital the following morning.

It sounds idyllic, and certainly Tuesdays were the most looked-forward-to evenings of the week, but it wasn't without its difficulties, especially when doctors forgot to pick me up or bring me back and I would spend a hectic hour rushing around campus houses and phoning hospital wards in a desperate attempt to find another car going in the right direction.

At a time when I most needed close fellowship my

need was met in the most wonderful way; the friend from England who had given me Guy and Jan's name in the first place wrote to ask if she could come and spend her Easter vacation from medical school with me in South Africa. In her letter she said, 'I'm coming out to see what kind of a mess I landed you in!'

Tania and I had been close friends for the past four years; God had sent her to me whilst I was struggling to overcome anorexia. Soon after I had made a commitment at a youth camp one of the people there prayed that as I returned home I would meet someone to whom I could relate and the following Sunday as I walked into Greyfriars Church for the first time I bumped into Tania – an extrovert Christian who had overcome anorexia! Within the next forty-eight hours we had struck up a friendship that has continued to grow by the year despite her being in Newcastle UK and my being in Newcastle SA!

Guy and I drove out to Newcastle Station at the dead of night to meet Tania. There were no street lights to guide us and sitting on a bench on the station was quite eerie. Apart from the constant buzz of crickets, it was quiet and only a few people wandered up and down the platform awaiting the arrival of the train for that evening which was still chugging its way down from Johannesburg at a snail's pace.

In the early hours of the morning the train arrived. No one seemed concerned that it was late; they could wait all night and day. Tania was leaning out of the window and waving; I rushed forward to greet her. It seemed an eternity since I had seen her and it felt completely unreal that she was in South Africa.

We talked all the way back to Madadeni and when we arrived Guy left us to carry on whilst he went to bed. There were things that could not wait until the morning and whilst we were both burning with excitement sleep eluded us. Tania started to throw things out of her case at random; somewhere at the bottom there were some parcels for me from my parents. Then she passed me a carrier bag; inside was a present from her. I pulled the handles aside and peered down; it was full of Twix and Star Bars. How my body had been craving chocolate! I had written to Tania and asked if she would bring me a Twix or Star Bar, but I never expected a carrier bag full of them! We both sat back and burst into fits of laughter and Tania said, 'I'd do the same again for you just to see your face – it was an absolute picture!'

On that note we decided that sleep called and we went our separate ways until morning.

The following days were spent working at the hospital. I had jobs to get on with and Tania, as a medical student, was interested in speaking to doctors and observing the wards. Then, work put aside for a few days, we went out on an adventure that had more surprises than we had bargained for!

We had arranged to do a set two-day trail in a part of the Drakensberg Mountains owned by some farmers not far from Newcastle. With packs on our backs and strong walking shoes we set out on the trail, which in the leaflet had been described as 'fairly tough'. That was an under-statement! We scrambled over rocks, panted up hills and slid down mountainsides. When our water-pots were empty we listened for the welcome sound of a trickling stream or waterfall and would rush in anticipation and ever-increasing thirst to scoop up the ice-cold refresh-ment into our hands. There was little time for rest as we had been several hours late setting out and darkness was quickly approaching. I would have sat around for hours resting my weary body but Tania recognised the urgency to keep on the move.

When I was ready to die and thinking we still had two kilometres to go, we stumbled across our overnight point – an open cave, firewood and pile of hay. From the top of the cave water dripped rhythmically into a bucket below. We breathed a heavy sigh of relief, no more walking until tomorrow; I sat down whilst Tania went to look for the hut. For what seemed eternity I sat on a wooden log and stared at the mass of trees knitted together in the valley. Nearing dark, Tania returned.

'I can't find a hut anywhere,' she said. 'Have another look at the instructions.'

I read aloud the leaflet on the trail. 'Overnight point – firewood, hay, water bucket and kettles.'

It said nothing about a hut anywhere – we had made an assumption that there was somewhere to sleep when in reality we were to spend the night alone under the stars amongst baboons! I chuckled to myself as I thought of the conversation I'd had with the organisers at the time of booking the trail.

'I'm not very happy about two girls going by themselves,' the lady said. 'You see, nothing locks.'

I envisaged a battered wooden hut without a key.

'And I think you might be frightened; no one around for miles, maybe the odd native and strange animal noises, baboons, and there are supposed to be leopard on the mountain slopes....'

A wooden hut, the vague possibility of leopard, baboons and natives was nothing compared with my experiences in Kenya: a flimsy tent, elephant, lion, buffalo and the Masai tribe!

'We won't be afraid, I'm sure,' I said with a convincing certainty.

Sitting in our new surroundings, feeling the vulnerability of an open cave and looking at the expanse of tangled undergrowth in front of us, I wasn't so sure about not being afraid, nor was Tania! Still, once we had more or less come to terms with the fact that the luxury of a hut was not a possibility, we set out to light a roaring fire.

'Were you ever a girl guide?' Tania asked me.

'No, were you?'

'No.'

'Shame,' I said. 'Still, it's easy to light a fire.'

Easy? Not so, when you are inexperienced and only have a pile of large logs. At the tenth attempt only a few matches left and a veil of darkness already falling upon the land, our hearts began to beat a little faster. It would be almost bearable sleeping in an open cave with the warmth and light of a fire, but sleeping in the cold mountain air in the pitch black was beyond a joke! A pile of hay was stuffed under the logs and the first spark took; then suddenly a mass of orange flames consumed the wood and all our anxieties were melted in the intense heat.

God was with us and we were very much aware of His presence. Tania received a beautiful picture of Him surrounding us in protection and we spent the next hour or so in praise and worship – singing, praying and reading from the pocket Bible we had remembered to slip into our pack at the last minute. Opening the Bible at random we stumbled across Psalm 103; the words were powerful and set the theme for our quiet time praise.

> *Praise the Lord, my soul!*
> *All my being, praise his holy name!*
> *Praise the Lord, my soul,*
> *And do not forget how kind he is.*
> *He forgives all my sins*
> *And heals all my diseases.*
> *He keeps me from the grave*
> *And blesses me with love and mercy.*
> *He fills my life with good things,*
> *So that I stay young and strong like an eagle.*
> (Psalm 103:1-5, GNB)

After a welcome meal of egg-mayonnaise sandwiches, carrot sticks, fruit juice and chocolate, we crawled into our hay pile and continued our time of singing. It was a most beautiful and precious time and one which left us filled to overflowing with God's amazing love.

During the night we woke up alternately every few hours and stoked up the fire. A cosy pair of socks on to keep our feet warm, one of us would pad through the dust and heave another log onto the rapidly-dying flames, then sleepily climb back into the hay pile. The amount of wood we had was perfect, it lasted until about 5 o'clock in the morning, when the sun shining through the mass of knotted tree branches told us that it was time to rise and make a move.

We were relieved that we had woken up in one piece but quite sad to be leaving our little cave and valley behind. There was plenty of icy water in our bucket to splash all over ourselves and bring us fully into the land of consciousness, and after a fairly leisurely start to the day we began on our homeward journey. The sound of the dripping water faded into the distance as we scrambled over rocks, through dense forest and out onto the open mountain slopes. The walking seemed easier the second day and by lunchtime we were back at the farm waiting to be picked up by Jan who was going to whisk us back to Madadeni for a quick wash and re-pack before catching a lift with one of the doctors to Durban.

It was dark by the time we had travelled for four hours along the road and freeway to reach Durban, but we were fortunate that our lift provided us with door-to-door service. We did not know the people with whom we were to stay; they were relatives of the curate and his wife from my home church in England and to my amazement were also known by Guy and Jan. A few days previously Jan had phoned to ask if Tania and I might spend Easter weekend with them. It so happened that they were planning on being away that weekend but were on a desperate hunt for a cat-sitter. Perfect! What more could we have wanted than a quiet weekend by the coast? They welcomed us inside and after a delicious meal showed us the ins and outs of the house so that if we woke up in the morning to find they had gone all would not be strange.

It turned out to be a beautifully relaxed weekend of lazy hours lying in the scorching sun beneath an avocado tree heavily laden with fruit and equally lazy moments wandering along Durban beach, the sand sifting between our toes and the waves bouncing in on the shore. If we weren't feeling the Indian Ocean beating against our bodies or swimming in the pool, we were ambling through African craft shops or, better still, paying a visit to one of the best ice-cream parlours I have ever seen, where such delicacies as banana-fudge and caramel-fudge ice-cream are listed in one's mind as irresistible!

Our last day in Durban provided us with plenty of entertainment and laughter to keep us going for a few days. Instead of catching the bus to the beach front in the morning we decided to walk. A little exercise will do us no harm, we thought, and a good hour later, suffering from dehydration, we reached the all-familiar sight of brown bodies surfing and sail-boarding on the over-active waves. We put our towels, clothes and picnic box down on the sand and ran into the warm water. Great fun until from a distance, and powerless to do anything, we saw the waves come dancing in on the shore and snatch away our lunch box and make an attempt at taking my trousers at the same time! Some kind gentleman seeing two ladies in distress made a hurried leap for the lunch box, which by now probably had wet, salty sandwiches inside, and placed it with the rest of our belongings a good distance from the incoming tide. By then our tolerance of sea and sun had reached its limit and it was time to take shelter in the cool of the shops.

We had chosen to spend our last evening seeing the film *Out of Africa* and turned up at the cinema for the early showing to discover that it was full and we would have to while away time in a restaurant until the late showing. Looking at our financial state, which proved us to be more pauper than rich man, we decided on a restaurant which had a set price and did not run the risk of the embarrassment of being short of cash! We came across an interesting-looking Greek restaurant and settled ourselves at a table for two. The choice and spread of food was amazing and every item appeared to be as appetising as the next. It was just as well that it was the type of restaurant where one was allowed to keep coming back for more! Tania and I sat eating and laughing until our bodies were more than satisfied and told us it was time to leave. There was not an atom of guilt over the amount we had eaten, and the fact that the pair of us were ex-anorexics made it all the funnier. We virtually rolled down the High Street to the cinema holding onto our stomachs, laughing all the way and saying, 'If anyone comes near my stomach I'll scream!'

We made it to the cinema to discover that everyone around us was smartly dressed, as though going to the theatre, and Tania and I were still in our sandy jeans and T-shirts. Feeling somewhat conspicuous attached to the end of a long queue, we decided to take a seat in the ladies room and time people as to how long they took to brush their hair and touch up their lipstick – one lady took fifteen minutes! At the end of that fruitless but somewhat hilarious half-hour, we found our seats and sat down to enjoy *Out of Africa*. The only problem was that I felt rather like a well-fed baby, ready for a good long sleep! All we needed at the end of the evening was for the taxi driver to get lost, swear blind that he knew where he was going and charge us more than we could afford. He managed to do just that!

13

Life is a painting

Life is a painting, a painting of scenes
Of the ups and downs and the in-betweens,
Of meadows full of the beauty of spring
And the bitter cold that winter can bring.

There are spacious fields filled with peace,
Hills to climb where striving won't cease,
A silver stream of endless love
And oppressive clouds which loom above.

There are paths leading to dreary dead-ends
Where you walk alone devoid of friends
And it seems so long, so hard, so unfair
As though there's nothing but blackness there.

There are forests where confusion lies
And earth's creation lives and dies,
Where trees stand majestic and tall
And rocks cause you to stumble and fall.

There are days when the sun breaks through
And shines on tears of crystal dew.
Where its golden beams of brilliant light
Add beauty to every place in sight.

So from life's painting a lesson borrow
Not to waste your joy or sorrow,
For these things are NEVER in vain
From them a soul, a heart you gain.

Whenever I hear people say that it is impossible fully to recover from anorexia, enjoy food and life and not feel guilty over eating, I recall the crazy day Tania and I spent in Durban. There is nothing special about either of us, and if we can make sea, sun and plenty of food into one of the most enjoyable days of our lives, so can anyone else!

Ironically, a few months after that incident I found myself only a stone's throw away from the Greek restaurant in Durban, visiting a young anorexic girl in hospital. Her parents and I had barely set foot inside the building when a social worker whisked us off into a side room. After a lengthy run-down on her condition, a heated discussion took place on whether a person can fully recover from anorexia. The way the hospital were handling her was good, with plenty of occupational therapy, but the sad thing was that she was being told that whilst she would learn to live with anorexia, she would never fully recover. The social worker insisted that she would always have an obsession about her weight and although she would be able to eat slimming foods she would never be able to indulge in such luxuries as coke, chips and chocolates.

'Why not?' I demanded. 'It took me a long time to get there, but I love coke, chips and chocolates now.'

Puffing on her cigarette, the social worker turned to me. 'Statistics,' she said, 'prove the failure to recover and the very great likelihood of relapse.'

'Blow statistics!' I said, 'each person is an individual. I believe one of the reasons so many anorexics fail to get better is that, certainly in the past, their condition has been misunderstood. They have been put into hospital, fattened up and sent home without their emotional needs or the root cause being dealt with. It's hardly surprising that they find themselves back at square one. Besides, if I had been led to believe that I would only half recover, I would probably have been content with half recovery and would still be nibbling at cottage cheese and lettuce leaves. Instead family and friends helped me expect nothing other than full recovery – life, not mere existence. If I am on the statistics anywhere it won't be down as 'recovered', it will probably be as a 'write-off', because I left hospital in a wheelchair and when last seen in outpatients, although slightly improved, I was still desperately underweight and distinctly anorexic!'

'I guess you're just an exception,' the social worker said.

'One of many,' I answered, 'including a good friend of mine!'

I went on to describe Tania's and my meal (and lack of guilt) at the Greek restaurant, our visits to the ice-cream parlour and how sea, sun and plenty of food had been the making of a really enjoyable holiday. Whilst the social worker seemed genuinely happy that I could relish such memorable moments, she none the less remained completely unconvinced that one day her young patient could be capable of the same. I tried telling her that she would have said the same of me when I was in hospital, afraid to have even a teaspoon of milk on some raspberries. Not even that altered her opinions and I decided that all of us in the smoke-filled room would have to remain with our own convictions concerning recovery.

With the quizzing over and mental exhaustion rapidly

setting in for all of us, at long last I managed to see the patient and have time alone to talk. I understood completely her fears and conflicts and hoped that, if nothing else, our half-hour together gave her the determination to win.

I was in Durban to give talks on anorexia in schools and churches as a part of the speaking tour Jan and I had arranged for my last month in South Africa.

My mother had flown out to join me for the tour which began with a two-day journey from Madadeni to Cape Town through the dry, barren landscape of the Karoo, leading into a dramatic area of beautifully craggy rock formations with colourful wild flowers. Luscious green vines stood out against a backdrop of grey-blue mountains.

Cape Town must be one of the world's most beautiful cities, nestling at the foot of the majestic Table Mountain, aptly named with its flat table top and its table cloth when the clouds drape over its sides. Great sweeping bays of white sand and blue seas skirt the city and in the Constantia suburb, where we stayed, the hillside was festooned with flowers of all colours as though someone had taken hold of a rainbow and scattered it on the ground. After rain had fallen, and as the sun shone brightly, trees and flowers sparkled like silver confetti sprinkled from the brilliant blue sky. The house where we stayed was appropriately named 'Silverhill'.

Hectic days of speaking were followed by intense evenings of counselling anorexics or their anxious parents, but in Somerset West we had a break of a few precious hours visiting friends, and this took me back in time and brought to life the stories and photos of my stay as a baby at The Two Fishes Hotel in Diani Beach, Kenya.

Beth and Allan now lived in Somerest West in a retirement village of sparkling white houses with balconies which had flowers of all shades showering down from them. They had brought much happiness to our family in the early days when we lived in Kenya, where they had owned The Two Fishes Hotel. Here we spent our last holiday before moving to England, enjoying the white sand, tropical blue sea, casuarina and palm trees and the sound of the surf beating against the shore. Twenty-two years had passed, I was only a baby then, and we had not seen Beth and Allan since. When my book *Puppet on a String* was published, which contained a short description of our time at The Two Fishes, I was determined to renew contact and send them a copy. We had heard that they had moved to South Africa, their country of origin, and with the aid of some ex-Kenya friends we managed to obtain an address. I mailed them a book and an old family photo. A few weeks later a reply arrived; they were delighted with the book, remembered my parents well, but had no recollection of me!

The day we spent with them proved to be memorable, with lunch at Gordon's Bay, a visit to the Stellenbosch Flower Show and views of the Hottentots Hollands Mountains, not to mention a large bowl of strawberries and cream – my favourite!

As we stood up to leave Beth handed me a shell from her collection as a gift. Little did she know that only ten months earlier an African man in Kenya had found in the sea an identical shell and said that he would clean it for me. I was to collect it later that day, but sadly I couldn't get to his part of the beach. When Beth handed me her shell, not only identical to the one that should have been mine, but also from Diani Beach, it was a beautiful reminder of how good our God is and how much He cares about even the smallest of details.

There were times on this tour when we felt we had aesthetic indigestion. We were confronted, as we drove, with so much beauty it was quite overwhelming. There was the unbelievable beauty of Knysna where mountain, sea, forests, lakes and flowers gather together to form an artists' paradise. Near here we stayed with a 'book crazy' couple on an idyllic Christian guest farm. Trudy drove us to this paradise to give us a break before an arduous formal speaking engagement, and at one point I wondered if I would make that talk for on our way home we found ourselves driving up a railway track where steam trains still run! It serves as both railway and road!

Formal ladies' gatherings were daunting enough but the thought of speaking to psychiatrists and other staff at a mental hospital, and the students of a multi-racial theological college, was enough to make me shake in my shoes. However these assignments in Grahamstown proved I had nothing to fear and I could not have had more welcoming and open-minded audiences. All were eager to learn more of how to help those in trouble. It was here that I received my first standing ovation – a deeply moving and encouraging experience.

In Grahamstown, too, it was immensely interesting to visit the Library for the Blind for whom Beth was translating my book into Braille. The sight of those great volumes with their tiny raised dots spelling out the words made me all the more grateful for the sight I now have, imperfect though it may be; and as we drove through the ever-changing scenery I thanked God for all His gifts to me.

We saw neat little groups of rondavels – round huts – in the Transkei (an independent black country) nestling together like newly-born kittens. This was obviously an area of peasant agriculture and subsistence farming. With roads like a hard and lumpy crocodile's back the country was undoubtedly poorer than South Africa; but there was a beauty and tranquillity in the scene with its cows and goats wandering on small well-kept patches of land, a beauty so often lacking in the large and prosperous cities I was used to in England. Yet I was grateful for my more comfortable life with its greater opportunities – the opportunity for example to spend this year learning so much and the opportunity to reach out to so many interested and interesting people on this tour. Even though by the time I reached the end of the tour in Durban, after over fifty-one talks in South Africa, I vowed I would never speak on the subject of anorexia again!

From Durban, my mother and I moved on to Pietermaritzburg to spend a quiet few days with my friend Carol and her family.

'There's just one thing,' Carol said, soon after we arrived, 'Would you mind speaking in church on Sunday night? Oh yes, and Africa Enterprise would like to make a video of an interview with you, and the psychologist phoned to ask if you could meet him and talk for an hour.'

'No problem,' I replied.

I decided I might as well give up the idea of escaping speaking on anorexia there and then! (I've had twenty years of giving talks since writing this!).

It was good to see Carol again and as soon as we set eyes on each other we laughed. This was the second time I had turned up on her doorstep, having said on a previous visit, 'I'll probably never see you again.'

That evening there was much fun and festivity and the chance to unwind after a hectic schedule. Carol's sister had just announced her engagement and feasting and speeches and a hysterical game of the South African version of Trivial Pursuit followed.

Sadly, all good things come to an end and not only was the time with Carol and her family about to draw to a close, my year in Africa was almost over too. My mother and I returned to Madadeni to begin to sort our belongings and send home in advance parcels of books and papers I had collected along the way.

It was hard to be saying goodbye to South Africa and I knew that in doing so I would be lucky if I managed to keep a completely dry eye, especially when leaving behind children of whom I had grown very fond, such as those I taught in both Sunday School and the junior youth group.

On the Friday before I left, the junior youth group chose to give me a surprise farewell party. I had heard that they were planning the party and so went and bought balloons to tie to the branches of the willow tree near the church. By the time the youth group normally started the children had put up a table under the tree and laid out plates of biscuits and cakes which they had bought from town that day. It touched me that they wanted to do something special, especially since for most the last thing they could afford was to buy the ingredients for a party, but it was obvious from the start that they had it all worked out perfectly.

Those organising the party asked everyone to gather around the table for tea; first they wanted to say grace, then there were beautifully prepared speeches and the presentation of a gift.

The last few days seemed to consist of farewell after farewell. Friends to say goodbye to, campus tea parties and a call from the rehabilitation centre for me to pop round and say goodbye to the patients who were keen to sing me some songs. At my last Hospital Christian Fellowship meeting the nursing staff also burst into melodious song and showered me with blessings and goodbyes. How I would miss the enthusiasm and liveliness of the Zulu people!

The day I was to leave sunny South Africa and head for the arctic north started bright and early. Guy and Jan drove my mother and me, and our overweight cases, to Newcastle Airport to fly to Johannesburg. In minutes we had been joined by the rest of the farewell committee, Mike and Rosemary and their younger son Robert, and Normonde, a Zulu friend.

Our too-heavy cases were excused by the airline and after photographs and tearful embraces, we climbed onto the little nine-seater plane, *The Spirit of Durban*. Mike turned to young Robert,

'How would you like to fly in that plane?'

'No fear!' Robert replied. 'One of the propellers isn't working.'

Sure enough, *The Spirit of Durban* seemed to lack the get-up-and-go! After a good five minutes of willing the plane to move, the pilot declared the battery flat and we all piled out! It would be two hours until the next plane but there was the added bonus of returning to the Rectory with Mike and Rosemary, and the chance for another cup of rooibosch (red-bush) tea – my favourite.

Finally we managed to make our way to Johannesburg and on to London. It was as we changed planes at Amsterdam that for the first time in weeks it felt like Christmas: dark and damp outside, trees with little white lights inside and a background of carols, which gave me a warm, glowing feeling.

In just over an hour we caught sight of London. My father was waiting at the airport and there was a blue sky and shining sun to greet us. It seemed strange to be back in England; it appeared small, cramped and cold and I felt as though I had woken up after a long dream. Looking around, things seemed strange and yet familiar and I had a feeling of disorientation. People were rushing around buying possessions, and I was struck by the sheer materialism and yet apparent discontent in people's lives. Africa had changed my whole outlook on life; it was difficult to put into words, but I knew that it would never change back again. Maybe 'a heart of stone changed into a heart of flesh' says a small part of it: a heart that knows a quality of life that seemed impossible even to imagine before. What the Lord gave me over those months was not a product of my emotions: it was a knowledge, peace and joy that passes all under-standing – something deep within that came from my developing relationship with Him.

In fact, so many of the experiences I had been through over the past few years had changed me, been a way of strengthening me against difficulties and enabling me to find a new way of coping with life; new purpose, meaning and joy. I feel that I now have a deeper understanding of my own emotions and a more healthy reaction to life's trials.

All that we encounter along life's way has purpose, whether good or bad, the snakes or the ladders. Or, as someone once wrote to me:

The breakings and pains in your life have brought, and will bring, healing and comfort and blessing to others. It reminds me of Mary's jar of ointment that was broken open. A precious and costly sacrifice, it brought a wonderful fragrance – firstly to bless Jesus, and then it filled the whole house, and so was a blessing to others. But equally it covered her with the lovely perfume. Her hair, her hands, her clothes, all of her radiated that beautiful fragrance. And so, through the breakings in our lives, Christ does a wonderful work – to spread His loveliness around, and to increase His expression of His loveliness in us. Our trials are not in vain!

Nicholaston House
Christian Retreat and Healing Centre

Helena Wilkinson is a part of the full-time, live-in team
at Nicholaston House, on the Gower peninsula in South
Wales. For further information on Helena's work and on
the work of Nicholaston House visit the websites:

www.helenawilkinson.co.uk
www.nicholastonhouse.org

The vision for Nicholaston House came about long
before it was purchased. Some thirteen years prior to the
House coming on the market in 1998, a group of Christians in a Methodist Chapel in a rural location on Gower
began praying for a place where people could get away
from the stresses of life to receive help and rest. They
believed that God would bring the centre into being and
that their role was to pray for it. Meanwhile a couple in
Surrey received a vision for 'a place where people who
are hurting could come and find space'. A series of God-
ordained events resulted in that couple, Derrick and Sue
Hancock, moving to Swansea, becoming involved in
Swansea City Mission, and the Mission purchasing
Nicholaston House. Other people who now work at
Nicholaston House had also had similar visions for a
residential centre for healing, and hence the House is
born out of the prayers, visions and longings of several
people who, over the years, have had a heart to see God

bring healing and restoration to broken lives.

In the entrance of the House are the words, 'In this place I will give peace'. People frequently comment on the peace they experience during their stay and the ways in which they encounter the presence of God in the House. As well as coming for rest, space and prayer ministry, people also come to Nicholaston House to participate in the week and weekend courses and retreats on offer. These events include prayer ministry, time out, creative activities, spiritual encouragement, and insight and support for those addressing a number of personal issues, such as eating disorders.

The location of the House itself is ideal for rest and renewal. Set in the heart of the Gower peninsula, an area of outstanding natural beauty, Nicholaston House overlooks the stunning Bay of Oxwich with its vast expanse of sand. In contrast, a country lane separates the back of the House from Cefn Bryn, where sheep, ponies, and cattle roam free across miles of open moorland. The whole area creates an ambiance of peace and tranquillity.

Inside the House, the downstairs comprises a sea-facing dining room, conservatory and lounge, a craft and bookstall, a purpose-built art and craft studio and two medium-sized conference rooms. The conference rooms can be opened up into one large room seating over 100 people.

Upstairs there is a lounge and a small chapel and library, as well as accommodation for around 28 people. All the bedrooms are en-suite (most are twin) and have colour television and tea- and coffee-making facilities. Many are sea-facing, and a passenger lift, as well as the main staircase, serve all. One bedroom is specifically adapted for those with disabilities – including wheelchair users. The disabled toilets, ramps and lift, make the House available to all.

The gardens, which overlook the sea, are designed to encourage relaxation and the House is a member of the

Quiet Gardens Trust.

If you would like to find out more about the work of Nicholaston House, then you can visit the website or write and ask for an information pack which includes details of the work, in-house events and resources.

Please send a large SAE to:

Nicholaston House, Penmaen, Gower,
Swansea SA3 2HL.
Tel: 01792 371317. Fax: 01792 371217.
Email: managers@nicholastonhouse.org